Be Great!

R. Dych

Praise for *The Great Ones*

*"With masterful story-telling reminiscent of Hemingway, Ridgely Golds-borough educates, enlightens, and inspires with his great new fable, **The Great Ones***. *You won't be able to put this one down and you'll enjoy every entertaining lesson along the way."*

Dr. Joe Rubino,
CEO, www.CenterForPersonal Reinvention.com
Author of ***The Self-Esteem Book***

*"Ridgely never ceases to amaze me. **The Great Ones** spells out the beauty of life when we have someone to look up to, learn from, and most of all mentor from. **The Great Ones** will no doubt be a bestseller as it depicts a relationship between a boy and an old man, which is, by all accounts, one of the most precious, soul-touching relationships known to mankind. **The Great Ones** will sit on my book shelf at the very front representing one of the most important growing experiences that life can offer . . . mentorship and guidance along life's narrow highway to success."*

Dr. Dallas Humble,
CEO, The Humble Group,
Author of ***Make It Happen, A Healthier You***

"I loved this story! Ridgely offers a beautiful parable about the power and magic of having a mentor who fans that sputtering little flame of self-respect. From a woman's perspective, I find his descriptions of both despair and delight quite moving, and he has an uncanny ability to capture the core of the human experience."

Maya Frost,
The Mind Masseuse

"There is an important group of individuals, men and women, who make a tremendous impact across the world. They are nurturers who give of themselves unconditionally, thus shaping the destinies of those they touch. They are called 'mentors' and come from the whole spectrum of the human

race. *The Great Ones* exemplifies, in a glorious way, the rags to riches tale—of the spiritual range—of a young boy who transforms his life by the touch of a mentor. We should all be so blessed as to have such a person in our lives . . . or to become one."

Lucia De Garcia,

President, Elan International

"*A Must-Read. Ridgely has done a fine job capturing a tale of growing into who we can all become, regardless of where we came from.*"

Nick Sarnicola,

Founder, Fusion Training System

"*With storytelling skills reminiscent of Richard Bach, C.S. Lewis, and Ernest Hemingway, Goldsborough's beautiful fable un-conceals one of the Universe's most valuable lessons—the power of taking one's life in their own hands. Couldn't put it down.*"

Russ DeVan, CEO,

Success by Design, Inc.

"*Packed with timeless wisdom, this engaging tale is a fast read with a timeless message. An inspiration for any age!*"

Don Fergusson, Life and Relationship Coach

Chief Architect of *The House of Intimacy*

Former President, Rust-Oleum Corporation

"*Wow! I just finished reading Ridgely's new book,* **The Great Ones.** *I read it in one seating because it was so captivating, powerful, artistic, and true. As a 10th degree black belt and Hall of Fame champion, I can concur with this powerful book. Every great person has a Sensei, Coach, Trainer, and/or Mentor that can help draw out the greatness. This book needs to be read by every living person who wants to excel in life. Be sure to get a mentor ASAP, if you need help finding one, check out www.mentorsclub.com!*"

Dr. Stan "Break Through" Harris

www.TheInternetMentor.com

www.DrBreakThrough.com

"Heart-wrenching in its innocence and simplicity. Uplifting in its lessons and perseverance."

Jayesh Patel,
Partner, Pumilia, Patel & Adamec, LLP

"There are few people I check in with on a regular basis that give me more pleasure, insight, and enthusiasm for life than Ridgely Goldsborough. He is part warrior, part Buddhist monk, part counselor, and always a loyal, intelligent friend. In his new book, **The Great Ones***, you get a clear vision of what it takes to be a great one, too—but, more importantly, you see what he went through in his own development. Make no mistake, this book is as much 'how to' as it is 'how I did it'—written so well that you'll forget you're learning from a Great One yourself."*

Scott Martineau,
CEO, www.ConsciousOne.com
Author of **The Power of YOU!**

"This book is a must read! **The Great Ones** *is a heartwarming, passionate story for anyone who needs reassurance of our human potential. Ridgely Goldsborough writes with clarity and candor, compelling you to read on. There is no putting this book down! It is warm and fascinating, and filled with priceless nuggets about how to design a wonderful life!"*

Kathleen Deoul,
Author of **Cancer Cover-Up**

*"***The Great Ones** *elegantly relates a message for all dreamers great and small. We should all have a friend like the Old Man much earlier in our lives!"*

Kevin Briley,
Managing Partner, Ascend Education

"A mentor is someone who has already walked the path we seek to travel. It makes no sense to travel without a map. Without question, a mentor is someone who can 'Pass It On.' Great work, Ridgely."

Gregory Scott Reid,
CEO, The Millionaire Mentor, Inc.
Film Producer, **Pass It On**

*"**The Great Ones** instills the essence of personal development on your mind without you ever noticing that you're being taught anything at all. This book gives you the unique opportunity to finally understand the truths you may have read about in all the other self-help books sitting in your library. Within minutes of opening it, you'll find yourself getting stuck in the story and growing into a more focused person with every chapter you read."*

Christopher Guerriero,
Author of **Maximize Your Metabolism**

"This book is a powerful exploration of character building and the impact of the significant people in our lives. I couldn't put the book down. A must read for those of us struggling with our past and also for those of us who mentor others."

Benita Creacy, CFP,
President, DC & Associates

"As a three-time Olympian, the message of never giving up resonates with me to the core. It is the difference between a champion and a wannabe, every time."

Ruben Gonzalez,
Author and Co-star of
the motivational movie, **Pass It On**

*"Ridgely just gets it. **The Great Ones** vividly displays how much we all need a mentor to light the way for us. Persuasion and manipulation are light years behind and Ridgely's book shows that clearly. You must have love in your heart for the people you lead. This book made me feel good."*

Dale Brown,
Former LSU Basketball Coach 1972–1997
Author of **Words to Lift Your Spirits**

*"**The Great Ones** is a book you absolutely deserve to read. Ridgely is a master at delivering the insight that will allow you to transform the way you feel about yourself so that you can produce larger results in life."*

Jeffery Combs,
President, Golden Mastermind Seminars, Inc.
Author of **Psychologically Unemployable**

*"This book has impacted me on many levels, steadily working down through the strata of my persona, like peeling away the layers of an onion. I am forever changed, and no longer willing to play small. My already dog-eared copy is not on the bookshelf, but rather nearby, where at any time I can open its pages and hear the voice of a wise mentor encouraging me to live a life of greatness, and reminding me that 'our choices define who we become, not our intentions.' This is an extraordinary book; a companion for living. **The Great Ones** will be judged a classic, read and reread for generations."*

Donna Cicotte Castro,
Founder, Coastal WealthBuilders

"A must read for anyone involved in nurturing the career of a protégé, a promising subordinate, or even a son or daughter . . . beautifully depicts the secrets of a successful life."

Rear Admiral James E. Koehr, USN (Ret)

"Ridgely provides an incredible story where the message is inspiring and the lessons are true. The turn of each page unveils a tale that will enhance your own magical journey in life."

Jeffrey St. Laurent,
Author of ***Already Ready!***
www.TrueYouNow.com

"Perhaps I was tired, perhaps it had been a long day, perhaps the emotions finally caught up with me. As I finished the last words of your book, I knew the message would be blatantly clear, but little did I know that the message would be that loud and clear. In every situation, there is an opportunity. Sometimes that opportunity is life-changing, sometimes not. But the compilation of all of our opportunities and the choices we make can change not only our lives, but other lives as well. Your book states, 'Not only do we not grasp a message fully the first time around, most of us need to hear the same thing over and over, from different perspectives and outlooks, before it will truly sink.' How true!

The story is a 'great one' and had deep meaning for me, because as I turned the last page, my mentor, my father, was sitting right next to me."

Laurie Lipsey Aronson,

President, Lipsey's

"Very powerful messages, delivered in a compelling and easy to read story—something for everyone—student, parent, manager, executive . . ."

John Tolmie,

VP Finance & Administration,

Visalus Holdings, LLC

"Mentors make up an integral part of any success system, particularly for those who wish to accelerate their learning curve and reach their goals more quickly and effectively. **The Great Ones** *paints a masterful picture of the development and acceptance of a mentoring relationship along with the building of stalwart character that inevitably accompanies such a noble journey."*

H. Laird Goldsborough,

President, Shaner Appraisals

"Life's successes are built on a foundation of key yet simple truths. **The Great Ones** *is both an entertaining and inspirational story that reminds us of these fundamental yet critical truths of how we can achieve success in our lives. I highly recommend this book."*

Neil Elmouchi, CLU, ChFC,

President, Summit Financial Consultants, Inc.

"Eye-Opening. Powerful. A Must Read for anyone who desires more out of themselves. Ridgely, thanks for a great piece of Success Wisdom."

John Di Lemme,

Author of ***Find Your Why and Fly!***

www.FindYourWhy.com

"Ridgely Goldsborough has a gift for making us look at the way we learn and how we pass messages on to others. This is a great read for mentors, students, parents, and professionals from all walks of life."

Cliff Michaels,
CEO, CMA Mortgage and Real Estate,
CEO, 1 Day MBA Success Training

"Ridgely's book is beautiful in both its writing and its message. A parable of character and strength emerging from childhood struggle thanks in part to the wise guidance of a mentor—a great message to share with old and young alike."

Graham Barrons Anthony,
CEO, Anthony Advisors
www.aadvisors.com

"In order to grow, we all need someone who at times believes more in us than we do in ourselves. We can wait until we have gathered all our own experiences from which to learn, or we can learn to listen to others who have already had those experiences! *The Great Ones* does an amazing job of relaying some of the best life lessons within a creative and relatable story. We all have 'the Boy' within us, and if you are willing to become the student, the lessons from *The Great Ones* will change your life."

Blake Mallen,
CMO, ViSalus Sciences

"Very entertaining read! Powerful lessons that teach about our own uniqueness and the endless possibilities we all have if we simply seek."

Todd Falcone,
CEO, www.ToddFalcone.com

"A must read for those of us engaged in the pursuit of greatness. Ridgely masters the process of mentoring through storytelling. He encourages us to seek a mentor and, in turn, become one."

Winnie Hart,
President and Creative Director,
The H Agency

"Unlike many inspirational speakers and writers, who decide what you should want, when you should want it, and how you should get it, Ridgely strives to help you identify your personal hopes and dreams, whatever they are, then gives you the tools to turn those dreams into reality. Ridgely has a deep respect for each individual, and as far as I can see, doesn't have a selfish bone in his body. His newest book, yet again, speaks of giving of oneself to uplift and guide those who are struggling to find their way."

Jaye Lewis,
Author of www.EntertainingAngels.org

THE
GREAT ONES

A Business Fable

*The Transformative Power
of a Mentor*

RIDGELY GOLDSBOROUGH

WILEY

John Wiley & Sons, Inc.

Published by John Wiley & Sons, Inc., Hoboken, New Jersey

Published simultaneously in Canada

For general information on our other products and services or for technical support, please contact our Customer Care Department within the United States at (800) 762-2974, outside the United States at (317) 572-3993 or fax (317) 572-4002.

Wiley also publishes its books in a variety of electronic formats. Some content that appears in print may not be available in electronic books. For more information about Wiley products, visit our web site at www.wiley.com.

Library of Congress Cataloging-in-Publication Data:

Goldsborough, Ridgely, 1960-
  The great ones : the transformative power of a mentor : a business
fable / by Ridgely Goldsborough.
    p. cm.
  Includes bibliographical references and index.
  ISBN 978-0-470-48594-1 (cloth)
  1. Mentoring in business. I. Title.
  HF5385.G65 2009
  658.3'124–dc22

                                        2009021668

Printed in the United States of America

10 9 8 7 6 5 4 3 2 1

Dedication

*First and foremost, this work is dedicated to Aaron Young,
my personal mentor and as trusted, compassionate, and
giving a friend as any person could ever have.*

*Your impact on me and the thousands I have the privilege of
serving will be felt for generations. Furthermore, the insights and
ideas contributed to this book make it what it has become and,
though I may bear the title of author on the cover, we will
always share in its triumph as knowing collaborators.
I could not have done this without you.*

*Second, my profound gratitude extends to my spiritual mentor,
Dr. Daisaku Ikeda, who continues to exemplify a quintessential
and remarkable life of service to others . . .*

*Last, I salute all who embrace mentorship, both as guides and
students. May our legions grow and turn into legends.*

The world needs a few more dedicated heroes.

Contents

Contents

Appreciation

Special thanks to my wife, Kathy, whose tireless daily support gives me the time and space to do this work. Without her efforts, love, and encouragement, none of this would be possible . . .

Thanks also to our four children, Jennifer, Melissa, Linus, and Camille, who help me smile and keep me young . . .

Acknowledgments

Much gratitude to Laird Goldsborough for his unbending ear, my brothers and sisters, Moms and Dads, cousins, and adopted family, for sticking with me through a tortuous emotional process.

Deep, heart-felt appreciation to Mark Barlow and all the other Akayama Ryu Jujutsu Senseis and fellow warriors, for every hard fall, locked joint, cracked rib or nose, or whatever. May the forging, much like our gratitude, never stop.

A huge salute to the Park Rangers who keep Johnson Beach, my lab, in pristine condition—thanks to you all.

Special thanks to Kyle Wilson, a great leader, mentor, partner, and friend.

This work could not have been completed without the mentorship of my Soka Gakkai family and comrades, too numerous to mention in full, though with much appreciation to:

John and Valerie Astin, Matilda Buck, Michael Cantor, John and Harumi Galligan, Trish Garland, Ethan Gelbaum, Frank Hatcher, Beverly Jermyn, Jeff Kriger, David Lehane, Greg Martin, David Martinez, Ian McIlraith, Gary Murie, Frank Nakabayashi, Loretta McNair, Danny Nagashima, David Pole, Michael Riggins, Richard Sasaki, Cliff Sawyer, to include only a few. All are greatly appreciated and motivate me every day to serve and contribute.

Foreword

I remember in detail the day the Girl Scouts showed up at the front door of my house.

"We already have a freezer full of cookies," I told them, which was not true.

"Thank you so much for supporting the Girl Scouts," the young ladies said with bright smiles.

The reality was that I did not have the two dollars in my pocket to buy any. I was disgusted with myself—a grown man with a family, at age 25, who couldn't even scrounge together a couple of bucks for the Girl Scouts.

Then I had the great fortune to meet my mentor, Earl Shoaf, and, over the next five years, he taught me philosophies and ways of viewing things that helped me completely turn my life around. I honestly have no idea of where I would be without him.

When it comes to success in life, there are few relationships on earth that will ever have a greater impact than that of a mentor, and the good news is that you don't have to meet them in person. A mentor can come from books, from audio programs, from seminars, and in person. Remember, the student seeks out the mentor, not the other way around.

The Great Ones portrays a beautiful example of mentorship between a young boy and an old man—one that in many ways reminds me of my own relationship with Mr. Shoaf. Read it, absorb its philosophies, and, most importantly, seek out mentors for the rest of your life.

I wish you a most prosperous journey,
Jim Rohn
Entrepreneur, author,
and motivational speaker

Book 1

The Inquisition

"If you're going through hell, don't stop."
—Brad McLain, Minister

Prelude

People ask me how it is that, hovering around the half-century mark, I continue to practice *Akayama Ryu Jujutsu* (Red Mountain Style), an aggressive, hard-core martial art, in which I am consistently upended, slammed to the ground, choked, and have my joints locked and stretched by men and women half my age or less—all of whom routinely give me black eyes, a busted nose, or a couple of broken ribs.

Not surprisingly, the ultra-successful never question this extreme behavior.

They understand the Code.

Rules, regulations, and universal laws apply to all of us at all times. That—coupled with awareness and disciplined thought (or lack thereof), repeated action, and execution—determines the degree of our ultimate success. More than simple lessons or teachings, these laws make up a Code that, if adhered to, will inevitably lead to immense success and that, if ignored, will with equal inevitability lead to failure. After conducting over 200 interviews of millionaires and billionaires, the rules of business engagement remain unerringly constant, to the point where, after the hundredth interview, I grew to expect certain answers with

Prologue

Torredembarra, Spain, 1964

The Boy heard the scuffle from his bedroom at the end of the upstairs hallway.

His mother and father screamed at each other—not surprising to him as it happened almost daily, though the routine of it seldom masked the pain that tore at his heart.

As usual, he burrowed his small body into the covers and buried his head beneath his pillow, as far into the recesses as he could hide.

Underneath the anger and the angst lurked that other familiar feeling—fear.

"Will he come for me next?" he thought to himself.

Quietly, he began to hum.

few surprises—a fact that should be comforting to us all. Follow the Code and succeed. Don't, and you may as well buy a lotto ticket—as your chances at hitting the big time will be about the same.

Note that you will find no secrets revealed here, only time-tested canons and proven precepts assembled to provide a blueprint for anyone to flourish in any business. The key lies in each of us—our ability to understand, embrace, and follow these rules in whatever the endeavor.

This book is about you, and me, and anyone with a dream and a desire to do whatever it takes to make that dream happen. The myriad success stories from people of all walks of life repeatedly demonstrate what is possible when preparation—learning the Code—meets opportunity—a condition that manifests often to the prepared mind.

This is a business book coupled with a business fable that is designed to drive home the principles of the Code. It is focused on economic success, largely because the concept of prosperity, as my mentor pointed out, can be elusive. If someone asks you: "How is your health?" you might respond: "Oh, fine." Does that mean that you can slip on a pair of running shoes and knock out a 10K, or that you rolled out of bed with your customary lower back pain and knee aches at bay? If queried: "How is your relationship?" you might reply: "Oh, good." Does that mean that you wake up after a restful sleep to gaze lovingly into the closed eyelids of your forever partner, or that you managed to sneak out of the house that morning without being yelled at? In other words, your answer is highly subjective in both cases.

Chapter One

Altafulla, Spain, 1969

"He beat me again," the Boy muttered as he climbed onto his customary perch.

The Old Man nodded, his ancient, twisted hands resting lightly on the tall bamboo fishing pole anchored in the rocks between his feet.

". . . For no reason," the Boy added. "It's not fair."

The Old Man nodded a second time.

"I don't know about fairness," the Old Man began, in a deep, gravelly voice. "It seems to me that all of us are dealt cards, both good and bad. Some learn to play theirs better."

Out of habit, the Old Man pulled lightly on the line that stretched flaccid into the purple and black waters of the Mediterranean. Nothing.

"He hit her, too," the Boy continued. He wondered when he had started calling his father and mother "him" and "her." It didn't matter. The Old Man understood. The Old Man understood most everything.

"You must have done something," the Old Man admonished. "You usually do—though even in that, you have a choice."

Financial prosperity can be more readily measured.
Is your bank account flush or not?

Do you make more money than you spend, enough to actually accumulate something?

Are your assets growing or diminishing?

In this work, we focus on financial prosperity because it is tangible and hard to dispute, though I believe that the many lessons discussed apply equally to all aspects of life.

Today's Great Ones do not necessarily strap on a quiver full of arrows, walk with a crossbow, and slip a long knife in their waist band. Their weapons, though no less powerful, have a more ethereal form: the unbending resolve of the single mom to give her children a better chance; the iron will of the injured athlete who, despite the pain, steps back onto the field of play; the grim determination of the failed businessperson who, regardless of another setback, reaches deep within for the strength to give it one more try.

Technology barely grants anyone an edge, as it is so readily available to all. Information is equally abundant, doubling every few years to the point of being almost overwhelming. Presently, more than ever, the greatest business weapon is the focused mind, which must be guarded, trained, and protected. The Great Ones train hard, seek out mentors, work with a team, and—most importantly—stand guard at the gateway to their minds—alert, ready, and open to any possibility, friend or foe, opportunity or threat.

The Great Ones bring together a unique blend of mental desire, a work ethic that leads to competency and the willingness to embrace repetition. They operate under a discipline to stay on a course that, based on the law of

The Boy smirked. "After he smacked her, I jumped on his leg," he said. "He kicked me away, into the bookcase. When he finished with her, he turned on me with his belt."

The Boy spoke with little emotion, as if giving a school history report.

"Stand and pull up your shirt, Boy," the Old Man stated. "I have aloe." The Old Man pulled his *navaja* from the folds of his wide, cloth belt and cut a long strip from the leaf in his bag. Gently, he smoothed the plant over the swollen welts on the Boy's back.

The Boy stiffened without a sound.

"He's a wounded bird, that one," the Old Man mused. "And a poor card player."

"He shouldn't take it out on me," the Boy complained.

"Nor should you incite him," the Old Man pressed back.

The Old Man had a way of pushing the Boy's buttons without ever making him wrong, exactly, or putting him down. It was almost as if he wanted to challenge the Boy, test him, and make him think.

Still, the Boy loved the Old Man more than anyone, and he loved Sunday afternoons more than any other day.

The breeze picked up slightly and caused white flecks of foam to crest over the tips of the dark swells that extended from beneath the rocks into an open sea.

"I have a new movie," the Old Man said, and the Boy's face lit up in an instant.

"It's about baseball," the Old Man added.

The Boy snapped his neck around. "What? Baseball? You don't even like baseball. You don't even know how to play."

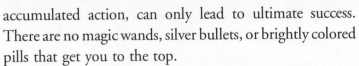

accumulated action, can only lead to ultimate success. There are no magic wands, silver bullets, or brightly colored pills that get you to the top.

I take no credit for the ideas or lessons contained on these pages. The project entitled "Modest To Millions"—which became a television show and internet phenomenon in multiple languages (see www.ModestToMillions.com)—granted me the rare privilege of conducting the previously mentioned 200 interviews (as of this writing) with successful women and men on the topics of success and wealth accumulation. I rapidly discovered during interview after interview that, although industries, titles, and experiences may vary, the underlying principles never do. In that discovery came a remarkable insight: If the principles are constant and unerring—and we have the capacity to learn and apply this Code—then anyone willing to do the work can become wealthy; and yes, that includes you and me.

Desire and disciplined thought, blended with the mastery granted by repetition and the relentless execution of proven systems, can yield only one ultimate result: total financial solvency and much more. Whether on the mat in the gym, in the boardroom, or simply on the road of business and life, I look forward to living the Code, side by side with you.

Stand guard. I wish you abundant prosperity, however YOU define it.

—Ridgely

The Old Man bobbed his head. "Not baseball exactly," the Old Man corrected. "Pedro recommended it. He said it was about dreamers, like us—about a guy who had a vision and built a field before he had players because somehow he knew they would come."

"That's crazy," the Boy snorted.

"Maybe, maybe not," the Old Man contested. "Sometimes you have to see things in your mind long before they can happen. We'll have to check it out for ourselves, find out what we discover.'"

The wind grew progressively stronger and caused the spray to rise high into the sky and sprinkle down on them.

"Can we watch it right now?" the Boy asked after a few moments.

"After the fishing," the Old Man answered as the Boy knew he would.

"Why?" the Boy grumbled selfishly. "You never catch anything anyway. In the years we've been out here, you've never caught a single fish. Why can't we go?"

The Old Man sighed.

"Ah, Boy. That's where you are mistaken. I had a nice bite earlier. If I keep on fishing, I am sure to catch a great fish. It's only if I quit that I might fail."

"Sure," the Boy muttered with a hint of disgust. "I'll believe it when I see it."

"Yes, you will," the Old Man smiled. "Yes, you will."

A Note on How You Can Best Benefit from this Work—

You will rapidly discover that this piece is actually two books in one: the first, a work of nonfiction based largely on objective analysis through field research gathered over years of interviews; the second, a fiction piece that brings to life the concepts that make up the Code.

The nonfiction part graces the left-side, a place for logic and reason. The fiction comes alive on the right, where nonlinear emotion has a free reign to experience and reach the subconscious through feelings.

As you undergo this journey of self-exploration and analysis, ask yourself how the issues that surface pertain to you, your business, and your life. The left-brained analytics will likely read the lessons straight through or in parallel with the story, while the right-brained creative types will blaze through the story and HOPEFULLY (please do) return to take a glance at the lessons. In either case, be courageous, for the ultimate beneficiary of the process will always be you. As with all things, our return will be determined by our investment.

To further cement the edicts in the Code, the chapters that most closely illustrate or exemplify a particular mandate are referenced after each one.

Learning and internalizing of the Code can be likened to fitting together a master mosaic, a piece here, another piece there, each granting greater understanding for the previous piece with each new one that takes its rightful spot. The speed with which the whole takes shape will

Chapter Two

The Boy heard him grab the iron railing and stumble up the stairs.

"Keep your breathing steady," the Boy willed himself. "Maybe he'll leave you alone," he thought without much hope.

His bedroom door opened and the stench of cheap *Priorato* filled his nostrils.

"Get up," his father ordered. "I know you're not asleep."

The Boy scrambled down from the top bunk and quickly headed toward the door in hopes of sparing his little brother huddled below.

No such luck.

"Both of you," came the command. "Downstairs."

The Boy and his brother took their positions on the marble tile in the living room with the Boy closest to his father's chair to act as a buffer. They stood at attention in their underwear, waiting. A half-empty carafe of local plonk squatted on the coffee table next to the tumbler that his father used as a wine glass. The Boy knew it had been filled and emptied more than once.

"Where was your mother this morning?" he demanded.

"At the market, I think," the Boy answered.

"You think?" his father continued. "But you don't know."

"No, sir." The Boy knew to keep his answers short.

vary, though the outcome will never be in doubt if you persist. You are the architect of the ultimate masterpiece.

Introduction

Since the beginning of community and the birth of commerce, men and women across the globe have sought to codify the rules for successful free enterprise. For hundreds, even thousands, of years, these rules passed only through generations of merchants and secretive banking families that often sought to manipulate both governments and the general populace for their own financial gain. With an increase in world trade and the rapid advancements in communication, this veil of secrecy began to lift at the beginning of the last century. Business giants and titans of industry allowed outsiders to step into their inner sanctums and sit in on meetings, watch them operate, and ask questions about their actions.

By the end of the millennium, these magnates' hesitancy in sharing the principles that governed their decision making had all but vanished. Still, for many financiers, the values that drove their behavior lay deeply ingrained and surfaced only through stories and anecdotes, or in bits and pieces over a dinner or in a rare moment of down time. Only a comprehensive study could clearly classify the fundamental rules of conduct that have proven repeatedly to drive success, particularly on a large scale.

After hundreds of hours of interviews over a protracted period, certain principles stand high above the

"'No, sir' you don't know or 'no, sir' you don't think?"

"No, sir, I don't know, sir."

The man curled a fat hand around the glass's rim and held it in his lap.

"Why do you 'think'? How do you know she got out of bed?" The charade went on.

"We had fresh vegetables at lunch," the Boy responded. "Sir," he added quickly.

"Where were you this afternoon?" He picked up his wine, pursed his lips, and drained the glass.

"I went to get her medicine at the *farmacia*."

The Boy's back began to cramp.

"Straight there and back?" The interrogation dragged.

"Yes, sir."

"And you never saw her walk by?"

"No, sir."

The Boy made no expression, gave nothing away. He simply stood in his boxer shorts with his arms at his sides.

"Do you think I'm as stupid as you?" The father reached for the carafe.

"No, sir," the Boy said softly.

"What's that?" the father grunted. "I'm not sure I heard you."

"No, sir," the Boy repeated a little louder.

"'No, sir' I'm not that stupid, or 'no, sir' I'm not as stupid as you."

The father pressed. The Boy held back. To engage him too early would only make it worse.

"No, sir," the Boy said again.

"That's it?" the father uttered, more fact than question.

rest. These have been brought together, revealed, and integrated into a single, concise Code.

Unlike how-to manuals that focus on the processes and specifics needed for a particular venture, the Code sets forth the general mandates for success in any business, regardless of culture, language, or industry. They have not—nor will they ever—change. The difference lies in the fact that now, unlike ever before, the barriers to their applicability have disappeared. Anyone can learn them and apply them. Those who do, as the forerunners and predecessors before them, will join an elite group and earn the right to be called The Great Ones.

"Yes, sir." The Boy knew the futility of trying to reason. He knew when to wait and when to provoke. He knew the beating would come shortly and didn't care. The words left far deeper scars.

"You better not lie to me, boy," the father barked.

"No, sir," the Boy parroted.

"Didn't you play *futbol* in the square?" The father's voice began to get agitated.

"No, sir," the Boy repeated, aware that the end drew near.

"You know you did not come straight back, and you're just not telling me. She said you could, despite what I told you, and you're protecting her like you always do."

The Boy watched the control slip, almost immune. Any moment now . . .

"So that's it—you're not going to tell me."

"No, sir," the Boy mumbled.

"Go get the belt," the father ordered. "And you better make it quick."

The Boy ran to his father's room, passed his mother hooked to her oxygen bottle, opened the top dresser drawer, and pulled out the brown leather belt, smooth on one side, rough on the other. He ran back and dropped it on the table next to the carafe.

He stood in defiance, the hatred flashing through his eyes.

"Turn around," his father commanded.

The Boy failed to move.

His father pushed himself up from his chair, took the belt in his left fist, and slapped it into the palm of his right.

"Turn around," he said again, "or you'll get it across your face."

The Code

I. *Thou shall make a decision and a commitment.*

II. *Thou shall conceive and execute a plan.*

III. *Thou shall take full responsibility.*

IV. *Thou shall embrace patience and temperance.*

V. *Thou shall act with courage.*

VI. *Thou shall cultivate passion.*

VII. *Thou shall exercise discipline.*

VIII. *Thou shall remain single-minded.*

IX. *Thou shall demand integrity.*

X. *Thou shall let go of past failures.*

XI. *Thou shall pay the price.*

XII. *Thou shall at all times persevere.*

The Boy slowly, purposefully, tauntingly turned and put his hands on the staircase. He spread his legs, braced himself, and mentally shut down.

He cried out when the first lash cut his skin—not because it hurt, but because he knew that unless he screamed the beating would go on until he did. Each time the belt bit into his back he yelped. His little brother started to whimper.

"You shut up," the father yelled, "unless you want me to give you something to really cry about." He waved the belt in the air.

The Boy sniffled anyway, ignoring the command, part of the game. If he stopped too soon, the beating would go on, even though he felt little pain. Eventually, the father tired, flopped into his throne, and drank more wine.

"Go to bed," he said. "Both of you."

The Boy and his brother scurried out of the room and up the stairs. When he closed the bedroom door, the Boy put his arm around his younger brother's shoulders.

"Don't worry," he urged, though the fearful sorrow in his brother's eyes spoke volumes. "It didn't hurt. I only pretended to cry so we could go to bed, like I always do. I didn't want him to hurt Mom."

The Boy climbed the ladder to his bunk, crawled under the covers, clasped his hands behind his head, and stared at the ceiling.

I. *Thou shall make a decision and a commitment.*

> *"If you don't make a total commitment to whatever you're doing, then you start looking to bail out the first time the boat starts leaking. It's tough enough getting that boat to shore with everybody rowing, let alone when a guy stands up and starts putting his life jacket on."*

—Lou Holtz

Chapter Three

The Boy marveled at the array of colors that cascaded downward each time he nailed a bulb dead center. Bright swaths of orange, crimson, and violet, along with bursts of indigo and evergreen, exploded into the sky, giving him his own personal fireworks show on demand.

Oddly, a slight deviation to the right or left caused little more than a pop and fizzle, though clearly the glass broke as he could see the tiny holes from his pellets.

Calmly and without hurry, he strolled through the deserted beachside resort, a ghost town in the heart of winter, and systematically shot out every streetlamp, pausing only to step into the trees at the first sound of the rare vehicle straying into the neighborhood.

He smiled when he scored a direct hit, grunted when he didn't, and promised himself with each miss to first pause, hold the gun steady, pull in a shallow breath, aim, and squeeze the trigger gently, exactly as his father had taught him.

"At least he's good for something," the Boy thought.

Explanation of Edict I

In today's marketplace, almost anyone can start a business with almost no effort and few resources. A person who has "people skills"—yet little organizational ability—can join a direct sales company for under $100 and begin selling their products or services. Someone with analytical and logical skills but no uniquely creative gifts can easily become an affiliate marketer on the internet and generate revenues by connecting other people's products with consumers—often with no start-up costs at all. A person who can both create and organize can acquire a domain name and build a website with an e-commerce platform for a minimal investment.

This ease of entry spawns a unique problem: easy in, easy out.

The road to business success is littered with the bodies of wannabe entrepreneurs who fell off the wagon as quickly as they jumped on. The vast majority failed to make a keen decision and certainly never made any kind of commitment.

And, as the Old Man shares with the Boy in the business fable portion of this book, those who make decisions slowly and change their minds quickly most often languish from one defeat to another. Those who decide quickly and change their mind slowly, on the other hand, succeed with far more frequency. What's the difference between these two?

The answer is simple: commitment. In the first case, the decision more closely resembles a whim or a fancy that disappears at the first sign of adversity, in favor of another

Chapter Four

The Boy flailed his arms in obvious debate.

"That's easy for you to say, old Man," the Boy debated. "You can do anything you want. I can't."

Instantly the Boy wondered if he had gone too far, if he had crossed the boundaries of respect. He swept his eyes across the sea before him, the lazy, undulating waves that signaled a calm day, and waited.

The Old Man tapped his finger on the weathered cane directly above the archaic, equally weathered reel, as he did sometimes before speaking. After a long while, he broke the silence.

"You see that pond of water gathered over by the spout?" The Old Man gestured with his head. The Boy nodded.

"Go to it and put your hand in it," the Old Man directed.

The Boy glanced at him as if to question, got off his perch, and walked across the rocks. He knelt down and placed his palm below the surface of the tepid water and looked up.

"Now take it out," the Old Man continued. "What do you see?"

"What do I see where?" the Boy asked, unable to contain his annoyance.

equally whimsical idea. In the second case, the decision carries with it the commitment to stick it out, to do what it takes, and continue on—regardless of circumstance. Even during harsh economic times—when more rapid change may be necessary—those decisions always carry the initial dedication with them: the promise to keep working, to keep analyzing, and to keep adjusting as needed.

Both the decision and the commitment require an active, ongoing choice with a continued life-force that backs them up. Neither of these exists in a passive state. In fact, the word *decision* comes from the Latin *decisio*, which means "a cutting short"—a cutting short of looking, considering, analyzing, and inaction, and a consequent move to action. The word *commitment* stems from the Latin *committere*, which translates as to "bring together and send"—to bring together all of the analysis, consideration, and factors that went into the decision and, again, to move into action.

The process of deciding begins the flow of energy in the direction of an objective; the process of committing ensures that this energy keeps flowing. As business philosopher Jim Rohn often states: "How long should you try? Until . . ."

. . . until your persistent commitment leads you to the desired result.

By contrast, the word *mediocrity* originates from the Latin *mediocris*, which means "of middle quality, indifferent, ordinary, commonplace." While a business person might easily "fall under" any of these definitions, no one "falls into" greatness.

"In the water," the Old Man replied calmly. "What mark did you leave?"

"I see nothing," the Boy retorted. "I didn't leave any mark."

"Exactly." The Old Man stopped until the Boy returned. "Most people leave that same mark with their lives—none at all. They chase idle, self-indulgent pleasures, complain about everything, and spend their existences addicted to their own importance. In the end, they leave as big a mark as your hand did in the water."

The Old Man reflexively tested his line.

"What does that have to do with me?" the Boy queried.

"Only a few wake up, Boy," the Old Man said with a steady, forward gaze. "The world is full of people trapped in their own pettiness, people who place another brick on the wall around themselves—a wall of their own making that grows taller and thicker each day with every careless word and deed—until they wake up one day old, tired, and resigned to a fate of mediocrity—bitter and full of blame. Let others lead small lives, Boy, not you."

The Boy sensed more to come and held his tongue.

"It is easy to destroy and much harder to build."

The Old Man switched hands on his pole. "Do you remember the great storm of last winter? What took many men years to construct was brought to the ground in a single night. It is the same with affairs of the heart. What might take a decade to create can be dashed into oblivion with one thoughtless comment, one act without consideration of consequence, one selfish moment. We must all consider what we value most and what we will do to protect it."

First, make a decision. Then, give that decision its value by making a strong commitment to it.

As the Code will define, the rest will naturally follow.

Reference Chapters: 6, 12, 18, 32, 36, and Epilogue.

The Old Man turned toward the Boy and then cast his eyes out to sea. "I heard about the lampposts," he said quietly. "Just because you didn't get caught, doesn't mean that people don't know who did it." The Old Man paused. "I felt great sadness when I found out." He paused again. "I thought you were better than that."

The Boy shuddered involuntarily as the Old Man's words pierced him to the core like a stiletto. His insides flipped upside down, his teeth ground shut, and his face turned into an ugly mask that fought back the swelling tears he tried to prevent. Rage and shame vied for center stage, only to mask the deep, numbing pain that churned within and paralyzed him—all except the renegade tears that snuck down his cheeks and tasted of salt.

To disappoint the Old Man, his best friend—in many ways, his only friend—hurt far worse than the sting of his father's belt. He felt nothing and everything all at the same time: nothing inside, everything outside, the light breeze across his temple, the hardness of the rock below his buttocks, the jagged crags beneath the soles of his feet, and, mostly, the rhythmic breathing of the Old Man he dared not look at.

The Boy heard the solitary cry of a lone seagull and watched it land in the dark waves that flowed incessantly, each unique and yet every one the same in their rapid, transient passage, as if they echoed the Old Man's thoughts on the impermanence of things.

Side by side they sat, the Boy in a maelstrom of emotion.

The Old Man stood when a fish struck his bait and let the line run before sharply jerking back on his pole. After a moment, the line went slack. Without words, the Old Man calmly stepped back and resumed his post.

II. *Thou shall conceive and execute a plan.*

"The person who makes a success of living is the one who sees his goal steadily and aims for it unswervingly. That is dedication."

—Cecil B. DeMille

The Mediterranean sun brushed its coppery reflection across the vastness of the sea until an afternoon cloud rumbled across the sky and blocked out the rays.

In an instant, the sun's copper painting disappeared.

Explanation of Edict II

Imagine that you owned a piece of land on which to build a dream house. Now picture yourself at a building supply warehouse purchasing brick and wood and wiring and a number of other supplies, which you load into your car or truck and transport to your lot.

After driving to your property you unload your materials and begin placing them hither and yon in order to construct the house.

Would you ever do that? Would you mix a batch of cement and start laying one brick on top of another, perhaps make a wall, and see where that takes you?

Of course not. It seems patently absurd.

And yet, that is exactly what most people do with their professional lives.

For the overwhelming majority of human beings, a career works like this. First you go to school and acquire certain skills, some more than others, much like the skills needed to install a carpet or wire the basement of your dream home.

Upon graduation and sometimes before, you purchase certain materials, a suit, a computer, a vehicle, a tool set, and with no thought other than to get a job, any job, you set forth into the world. Most jump at the first offer, at which point you instantly fall into someone else's plan, someone who has very little planned for you, and, as we all are, is far more concerned with their own success than with yours.

How is that any different than building a dream home without a blueprint or a set of properly crafted schematics?

Chapter Five

The Boy rested on the bench on the outdoor patio with his pellet gun across his lap. He watched the minute hand on the town square's clock tower tick its way toward eight o'clock, his appointed time to return home. He would wait until the bell began to ring before he went in, not a minute late to invite any punishment, nor a minute earlier than absolutely necessary.

He felt sick to his stomach. He remembered the exact moment an hour earlier when he shot the bird, the way the pellet struck its chest, the way it wavered briefly on the pine tree branch before it tumbled forward and fell to the ground, lifeless. He forced himself to go to it and look. There it lay in the burnt summer grass, gray and brown feathers swaying in the breeze, dead. It made him ill. He couldn't shake the nauseous, bubbling upset in his belly.

"I'll never do that again," he vowed to himself, then and now.

The bell started its toll. He forced himself to his feet, stepped through the front door, put his gun in the closet, and began to set the table with a sense of dread. He pondered how long it would be before his father made his way from his chair to the head of the dining room and began the inquisition. He hated the flashy, yellow book that sat on the sideboard in waiting, the repository of

In the end you wander through a cobbled together career that drifts from one plan to another, none of them drawn up by you—much like constructing one wall at a time in the hopes that the dream home will one day reveal itself.

As sure as the dusk precedes the night, that will never happen.

To succeed at anything, we must conceive and execute a specific plan, with clear deliverables, accountability, measurable results, time frames, contingencies, and regular reviews. The decision and commitment discussed in the first edict must then be followed by the conception and mapping out of a specific plan of action.

Years ago, much talk was made of one-year, two-year, and five-year plans. Forget all that. Global economics move so fast today that planning periods have been compressed. Now, to succeed at the highest levels, you need a long-term vision for where you want to be a year, two years, and even a decade away coupled with a 90-day, step-by-step action plan that will be reviewed and analyzed and re-made every three months.

Think back to the recession that began in late 2008. It came on so suddenly. that within less than six months, the entire global economy fell from record highs in most categories to complete turmoil. This can happen at anytime, to anyone, in any business. Today's free enterprise demands constant vigilance and adjustment. What used to last forever, now lasts a few months. The only way to watchdog and grow a business is with continuous planning, revising, measuring, and starting the same process again.

questions and answers of the hit TV show *Brain of Britain* that his father picked up on his last trip overseas.

Each night he would get a "lesson," a series of interrogatories from the book on a topic assigned the night before. The father would skim the questions, select the toughest ones, and start peppering away, waiting only for the mistakes to call the Boy "stupid" or "ignorant" or whatever insult struck his drunken fancy.

"At least we're having *chorizo*," the Boy thought, wondering how many people would eat the seasoned meat, stomach, and fat wrapped by a pig's intestine if they really knew its composition.

"Geography," his father began. "That's the order of the day—learn about the great big world, where diverse places are and all their neighbors. I loved geography as a kid."

"Yeah, right," the Boy mused in his head.

"Maybe you'll get to go to some of these places one day, Boy."

"Not if you're gonna' be there," the Boy promised himself. He said nothing.

"Let's see . . . here's a good one . . . tell me, Boy—where's Salisbury?"

"It's the former capital of Rhodesia," the Boy answered from memory.

"What's it called now?" the father continued.

"Zimbabwe," the Boy replied.

"Two for two," the father exclaimed. "Wow, maybe you're not so stupid after all." He flipped a couple of pages. "How about this one . . . give me the names of the countries that border Iran."

"Iraq, Saudi Arabia, Turkey, and India," the Boy guessed, knowing what would come next.

So what are the elements of a successful plan? First and foremost, a quick clarification: A plan that is not in writing is a dream, an idea, or a possibility for consideration and no more. Without for a moment denigrating the value of dreaming and brainstorming, these must be distinguished from planning. Planning involves the process of putting down in some written format the specific action steps, targets, and goals of a business, the results of which can be clearly measured and analyzed on a regular basis—and no less than at 90-day intervals at the most.

"Hmmm . . . two out of five—not bad if you're playing baseball, fairly pathetic anywhere else."

The father set the book next to his napkin. "Do you like being stupid or did you just not study today?"

"No, sir," the Boy muttered. "I mean, 'yes, sir,'" he corrected.

"'No, sir,' you don't like being stupid or 'no, sir' you didn't study." His father smiled his wolfish, sadistic grin. A small piece of chorizo stuck between his wine-stained teeth.

"'No, sir,' I'm not stupid and 'yes, sir' I did study—sir," the Boy added for emphasis.

"Maybe you've just been hanging around the ignorant local peasants too long," the father accused. "Like that ancient mariner that never brings in any fish. Maybe their ignorance is rubbing off on you."

It took all of the Boy's control to not react to the comment about the Old Man. He kept his eyes on his plate and grit his teeth.

"What's wrong with you Boy?" the father went on. "You seem even more pathetic than usual," he stated and chuckled at this own paltry joke.

"I shot a bird," the Boy mumbled. "It's dead."

The father spit out his wine in a huge guffaw. "Awww," he mocked in a fake baby voice. "You shot a little birdie-wirdie and now you're all upsetty-wetty." He laughed and laughed. Finally, he drained his wine glass and put it on the placemat.

"What you should do . . . ," he chortled, ". . . is shoot the obnoxious cats that keep getting into our garbage—make yourself useful with that gun of yours."

While entire books have been written about the art of the perfect plan, I would suggest that, at the very minimum, a solid plan must contain:

General—things that will not likely change with each rendition of your plan:

- A statement of your own or your company's core values, the characteristics that you stand for, and what drives your behavior.

- A statement of your key competencies—what you do well.

- A mission statement that defines why you do what you do and for whom you do it.

- A definition of what you want to deliver to the marketplace—what promises your company makes.

- Long-term goals that, while not part of the 90-day operating plan, help key the end game in mind.

Specifics—things that will adjust every 90 days:

- Action items—what specifically are you focused on for the next 90 days? What are your drivers?

- Precise targets—what are the goals for revenue, new customers, your product inventory, your cash flow, your profitability?

- Key numbers—what are you tracking that is critical to your business and its success?

- Clear accountability—who is going to be responsible for the action items that drive the business?

He paused briefly. "I'm serious. The next time you hear them out there, go upstairs, open your bedroom window, and start plinking away. Maybe we can take care of this problem."

The father leaned back with a smug, self-satisfied smirk.

"Don't worry, little Boy," the father went on. "It's not like the bird. You won't hurt the cats unless you pop them in the head. Aim for their back hip. If you hit 'em just right, their paws will splay out front and back and then they'll take off like jack rabbits so you'll know that all you did was sting 'em a bit, Mr. Sensitive-all-of-a-sudden."

The Boy started to rise. His father's voice froze him to the chair.

"Where do you think you're going, Boy," he bellowed. "We haven't finished our lesson and your mother's not here to protect you." He began to turn another page.

"Awww, hell, Boy," he stated. "Get out of here. You're so sad that you're beginning to depress my own self." He chuckled at his words again. "Get me some wine and clean up the dishes—and do it properly this time, unless you want a repeat of last night."

The Boy flashed back to the previous eve, when, a short time after midnight, his father barged into their room and dragged he and his younger brother out of bed. As they staggered downstairs, they discovered pots, pans, plates, cups, mugs, utensils, and silverware strewn across the living room, dining room, and office—literally every piece the house contained.

"When I say 'Do the dishes' that means wash, dry, and put them away where they belong," their father yelled. "Not wash and leave them dripping wet in the strainer by the sink. Now put them away properly," he ordered and sank into his chair.

Chapter Five   35

- A SWOT analysis. What are your strengths, weaknesses, opportunities, and threats? This is a particularly valuable exercise for new enterprises. What could go wrong? Where can you capitalize on your strengths? What could help you exceed your targets? What threatens not only the immediate achievement of your objectives, but also the very business itself?

Verne Harnish, author of *Master the Rockefeller Habits*, teaches a 90-day system centered around a one-page strategic plan that is revised and redone every quarter (this and other valuable resources are available on Verne's website at www.gazelles.com). I have been following this system for years and it is amazing how the items that make it to the page also manifest in the physical world.

At first, the benefits of the process lacked clarity. While I recognized the value of a written plan, only repetition and discipline in the making of it quarter after quarter coupled with an intrepid analysis of the results (or lack thereof in certain areas) revealed tendencies, trends, overarching flawed thinking, and areas that needed improvement—as well as the strengths that could be further taken advantage of. Over time the foundation gained solidity, the fundamentals grew deep roots, and the financial walls that protect the business and my family went up brick by brick. Here's the *major* upshot. Because the basics were handled and the house was in order, when a huge opportunity presented itself, with few distractions and the ability to single-mindedly focus, we jumped on it, as a result of which *Modest to Millions* has

The Boy and his brother spent 30 minutes under the watchful eye of their mother putting away every article in sight. Later, as his younger brother whimpered in his bed, the Boy sought to comfort him. "It wasn't that bad," he said gently. "It probably took him longer to put all that stuff out than it took us to put it away—and he didn't even hit us. He was just drunk."

Startled back to reality, the Boy pushed away from the table, stood quietly, fetched the carafe off of the coffee table, picked up his mother and fathers' plates, and escaped into the kitchen.

become a global success. In addition, with the financial house in order, those very walls can now weather virtually any kind of storm.

To further emphasize the absolute requirement of disciplined, repeated actions based on clear plans that are constantly scrutinized and evaluated, I should point out that my first attempt, a few years earlier, at bringing *Modest to Millions* to life yielded a paltry result. The idea alone—despite my best intentions, the resounding success of Napoleon Hill's similar work with *Think and Grow Rich* a century before, and the access through my mentor to titans of industry—was simply not good enough. It took repeated SWOT analysis through the one-page plan, repeated revisiting of goals and objectives, repeated affirmation of our intention and long-term vision, and repeated and sometimes painful review of the numbers—along with the daily slugging it out with distractions—to finally assemble the team that could craft and execute the plan that brought about our eventual success. We never caught a free ride or lucky break, nor did we need one despite my precedent wishful thinking.

In its most elementary form, a plan can be drafted on a sheet of paper, as has happened for centuries before the advent of computers. The key is to get it done and continue the process, quarter after quarter, which will rapidly paint a clear picture of the true state of your affairs—not wishes or intentions.

Each time after a setback, the Old Man counsels the Boy to reevaluate, reconsider, and start again more intelligently—in essence to plan, judge the results, and plan

Chapter Six

The Boy wore a broad grin as he scrambled up the outcrop—Sunday, his favorite day, on the rocks, his favorite place. The Old Man greeted him with a smile and reached into his pocket.

"*Quieres menta?*" he asked.

"*Gracias,*" the Boy answered as he took the candy and climbed onto his spot.

"Get any bites?" the Boy inquired, part of their ritual.

"One," the Old Man replied. "Didn't take but it will."

"You always say that," the Boy retorted.

"Because it's true," the Old Man claimed. "If I keep fishing, they will come, just like the man in the movie. He built the field and the players showed up."

The Boy glanced sideways at the Old Man. "That's in a movie," he smirked. "That's not real."

"Maybe." The Old Man tapped on his pole. "Though more often than not, it works like that in life. Can you imagine someone about to build a house who goes to the factory to buy bricks and cement and drives to their land and starts to pile one brick on top of another?"

"No," the Boy muttered. "Of course not."

"Why not?" the Old Man questioned.

again. This we must all do to attain success and, as will become clear, is a crucial piece to becoming a Great One.

Reference Chapters: 1, 6, 14, 15, 18, 26, and 31.

"Because they have to make a plan first," the Boy answered, half annoyed. "That's why," he added for emphasis.

"Almost," the Old Man corrected. "Except that there's a prior step before that." He paused to adjust his posture. "First they have to 'see' the house—the walls, the doors, the windows, the steps, the roof, and the chimney. They have to build it in their mind. Only when they can see it in full detail can they make a plan and finally begin to build."

The Old Man turned his reel twice before continuing.

"It's like the great strikers of Barcelona before a free kick. First they carefully place the ball on the pitch—just right—and begin to visualize the shot. Then they look at the goal, at the defense, and the position of the goalie. They see the ball rising up, sailing over the wall of defenders, and dipping down into the back of the net, too far for the goalie's outstretched dive. Only when they clearly 'see' it all do they drop back, take a few, precise steps, and strike the ball. They have to first see it in their mind before they can score on the field."

The Old Man's voice turned reflective. "Unfortunately, most people 'see' very little."

"What do you mean?" the Boy queried.

The Old Man gathered his thoughts.

"Most people get up in the morning and brush their teeth only to then drink the very same coffee that stains them. They cover blemishes with make-up and creams, hide their uncared-for bodies in clothes that someone else tells them they should wear, pile into their cars to drive to a job that they feel no passion for, and spend the week counting the days until Friday—another weekend and an opportunity to further distract themselves, mow their lawns, and moan about it. They spend more time designing

III. *Thou shall take full responsibility.*

"What we say and what we do
ultimately comes back to us.
So let us own our responsibility,
place it in our hands,
and carry it with dignity and strength."

—Gloria Evangelina Anzaldua

an annual vacation than they do planning their lives, become happy or sad according to a win or loss of a favorite sports team, get depressed when it rains, and angry when served overcooked vegetables."

The Old Man turned his head. "It's a small way to live, Boy, small and poor, in all senses of the word."

The Boy frowned and twisted the candy wrapper in his fingers. "Many people don't have much choice," he stated. "It's not like I can skip school any time I want any more than some people can blow off going to their job."

"Of course you could, Boy," the Old Man argued. "And you would suffer the consequences of that act as we all must." He stopped and glanced at the Boy. "And speaking of school—how's it going? I heard you had some issues."

The Boy crumpled the wrapper in his palm. "It's okay, I guess," he mumbled. "The teachers hate me because I get in fights sometimes."

"You spend too much energy being angry," the Old Man pointed out. "If you took that energy and applied it to your studies you might learn more, gain some confidence, and feel better about yourself. Then the teachers would treat you better. People gravitate toward others who are confident. It helps them feel more comfortable."

"That's easy for you to say, Old Man," the Boy spat. "You don't get beaten every day."

The Old Man looked long upon the water, as if the serenity shadowed in the waves would somehow flow to the Boy.

"Neither do you, son," he said finally in a calm and gentle tone. "You have many days without beatings, more of them in

Explanation of Edict III

Responsibility is defined as "the condition, quality, fact, or instance of being responsible . . ." The word *responsible* follows with a number of relevant definitions, including:

1. expected or obligated to account for something, to someone;

2. involving accountability, obligation, or duties;

3. answerable or accountable as being the cause, agent, or source of something;

4. able to distinguish between right and wrong and to think and act rationally, and hence accountable for one's behavior;

5. trustworthy, dependable, reliable; and

6. able to pay debts or meet business obligations.

If you run a business, you are expected to account for it—to yourself and/or others. It involves obligations and duties that must be performed in order for the company to flourish. You must be the cause or source for your firm's success; you must think rationally and differentiate between the right and wrong actions that drive it forward. For it to grow, you must become trustworthy, dependable, and reliable; for it to initially survive, you must meet your business obligations.

In other words, without exception, the definitions for the term *responsible* set forth a broad array of qualities needed for any major level of success, some of which address a mind-set, others that imply certain requisite behavior.

fact. The challenge lies in that you focus more on the beatings than on the good days and, as with all of us, you become what you think about most. Perhaps if you chose to concentrate on the positive, there would be fewer fights at school, less trouble at home."

"Yeah," the Boy grumbled, "like when his holiness is out of town on business. That's a positive for me."

"And many others, Boy," the Old Man shared softly, "the curl of a rose petal, the coolness of the sea, the sound of a bee feeding, the sweet taste of the *menta*, the love of your brother, the breeze on our foreheads, and the sun on our face. There are so many and they are everywhere as long as you open your eyes and your heart."

The Old Man put his hand on the Boy's shoulder.

"You must guard the gateway to your mind, Boy—and choose carefully what you allow in or what you give your energy to, for it will shape you and define you."

The Boy sat in silence. He stared at the brown, leather sandals that his mother bought at the local market on a rare day when she could get out of bed. Because they were new, they squeaked when he walked. He couldn't wait until they were broken in and silent, like the ones the Old Man wore. He swung his feet back and forth, smacking the rocks.

"How come you know so much, Old Man?" the Boy sought.

After a while, the Old Man spoke. "A long time ago, a special person taught me the difference between living and sleep walking." He paused to smile. "Ever since, I have chosen to live awake."

The Old Man squeezed the Boy's shoulder. "As you will, Boy," he added. "When you're ready."

In my favorite business book of all time, _Good to Great_ (and, yes, I highly recommend it), author Jim Collins describes _The Stockdale Paradox_—a condition that refers to a state of mind attained by Admiral Jim Stockdale while he was detained at a POW camp in Vietnam. Stockdale used this method of thinking to both save his own life and save the lives of many who followed him as the senior military officer in the camp. _The Stockdale Paradox_ dictates that one must: "Retain faith that you will prevail in the end, regardless of the difficulties; and at the same time, confront the most brutal facts of your current reality, whatever they might be."(Collins 86)

Despite the horrendous circumstances in which they found themselves, the plight of the POWs had an element of clarity that made the battle uncomplicated, definite, and defined. Withstand torture from the enemy, find a way to survive, and get out alive. The pioneers of any culture or land faced similar challenges—namely, avoid marauding thieves, figure out how to get through sub-zero winters, and stay away from bears.

Today's battlefield is much more subtle. We no longer fear for bandits along our roads or wild animals that live mostly on reserves; soup kitchens or other social programs keep most of us from starving. As a result, we have grown mentally soft. It is easier to have someone else tell us what to do than to figure it out for ourselves. We would rather play it safe than take a risk and expose ourselves to failure.

However, the Great Ones differ substantially in this respect. They _never_ place the onus for the demise of an enterprise on the government, the economy, a climactic

Chapter Seven

The Boy and his brother stood on top of the hill far above the church with their pellet guns resting in the crooks of their arms, just like the Texas Rangers on the western movie they had watched the night before.

They walked through the terraced orange and olive groves, up the rutted stone roads built in the time of the Romans, caught up in a world of make believe, covered wagons, plundered villages, burnings at the stake. On each knoll they stopped to survey the land below, acting as grizzled pioneers of by-gone days.

They plinked at pine cones and oranges and olive trees and anything that made an attractive target. Now, looking down from up high, they felt invincible.

"You wanna' play good guy, bad guy?" the Boy asked his brother.

"What do you mean?"

"Like the trackers in the movie we saw. We go hide, try to find each other, and whoever spots the other takes him out." The Boy's eyes lit up with his explanation.

"You mean shoot him?" his little brother stated in a fearful voice.

disaster, or any other outside cause. *Full responsibility* means just that. They are aware that, "I am the causal element that determines the success or decline of my business, to the point at which—if some tragic event beseeches me and the venture fails—it will only be because *I* did not prepare my team for such an eventuality. No excuses allowed."

As *The Stockdale Paradox* implies, true responsibility delves beyond bold statements and into the nitty-gritty. It asks, what are your numbers? How does your balance sheet look? Is the profit and loss statement in the black? If not, what's your burn rate and how long can you survive?

What can you do to extend that period or shorten your time frame to profitability? What are you going to do in the event of catastrophic occurrence A, B, or C? In other words, the business person must make continuous, honest assessments of the current condition of his or her enterprise, assets, and income-generating activities and, in so doing, find ways to marginalize weaknesses and optimize strengths.

To the extent that it is possible based on each person's circumstances, I recommend looking for an activity that fosters mental toughness—one whose completion goes beyond the physical and into a mental "victory over self" dimension. Run a marathon, bike 100 miles, swim a 5K, kayak down a white-water river—anything that forces us to dig deeper within ourselves for the strength that drives our very survival. In the Japanese martial art of *jujutsu*, two opponents square off with one objective—to take an adversary out, bury him or her into the ground, and subdue him or her. Then you get up, dust yourself off, and do it again. After

"Well, no, not really," the Boy faltered. "Maybe shoot the tree right next to him or the dirt at his feet or something like that."

"Sounds kind of dangerous," his little brother voiced, hesitant.

"It'll be fun, like in the Old West, every man for himself, survival of the fittest, take no prisoners, you know . . ." the Boy pressed his case. "Like hide and go seek except for real."

"Are you sure?" his brother pleaded one last time.

"Yeah, yeah, let's do it, and don't worry." The Boy slapped his brother on the shoulder. "Remember, the Texas Rangers . . ."

". . . always get their man," his brother finished, laughing.

They separated, and once out of sight the Boy tore down the hill and up the next one, into a group of pine trees where he could move around unseen. He felt exhilarated, his senses on full alert, his body alive and on edge. He could smell the resin in the trees and feel the moisture of the grass and the prickles of every pine needle on his arms.

Methodically, he worked his way through the mini-forest until he found the perfect place—three trees thick with needles all together. He knelt, peered through the gaps between the branches, and waited.

There.

He saw something.

Something moving in the boulders at the bottom of the hill.

Something or someone.

He inched forward to improve the scope of his view and wondered if he had been spotted.

There it is again.

Something moving from one boulder to another.

a particularly harsh throw, the struggle to face up another attacker looms far greater in the mind than in the muscles.

The business person faces the same struggle with responsibility. He or she wonders, what can I do to embrace the reality that every aspect of my business belongs to me—good, bad, ugly and everything in between, every day, 365 per year, no exceptions?!?

Each time the Boy suffers a beating—as well as after every transgression—the Old Man's first admonition, though often subtle, pushes him toward increased levels of taking responsibility—never sleepwalk, play your cards, don't give away your power, and so on. To the final lesson, the Old Man relentlessly drives this point home. The Great Ones blame no one; and no one that places blame will ever become a Great One.

Note how the Code builds on itself, from the initial decision and commitment to that decision, to the conception and execution of a plan that demands full responsibility from both conceiver and executor. This dynamic progression will continue to fuse together all elements of the Code, each supporting and adding strength to the others and acting in conjunction to form an unstoppable formula for success.

Reference Chapters: 1, 4, 8, 10, 20, 26, and 32.

Could it be? No . . .

Maybe . . .

Almost in a trance, he shouldered his gun, every nerve tingling, every fiber engaged. He took sight down the barrel, pulled his breath in slowly, froze, and pulled the trigger.

"Got it!" he exclaimed.

Suddenly, it was all wrong.

The scene played in slow motion.

The red burst on the rock, his brother's scream that wouldn't stop—the whole thing was wrong, horribly, terribly wrong.

He flew down the hill yelling, "No, noooooo, nooooo."

There he lay, his baby brother, on the ground with fingers on his forehead covered in blood, crying terrified, heaving sobs, and bleeding.

The Boy grabbed his brother in disbelief. "I'm sorry, I'm sorry," he repeated over and over in a daze.

"I need Mommy," his brother exclaimed between tears.

"What?" the Boy questioned, as if he hadn't heard the words, unable to take it all in.

"I need Mom," his brother repeated. "I need Mommy."

In that instant the Boy's guts turned from fear to panic.

"I'm dead," the Boy realized, "stone, cold, dead. He will kill me for sure."

Barely conscious, the Boy led his brother through the fields. His mind ceased to function—that same numb sensation that crept over him during a beating—as if his body isolated from his brain.

"What are we going to tell Mommy?" his brother said two or three times until the words registered and the Boy glanced at him.

IV. Thou shall embrace patience and temperance.

"Adopt the pace of nature: her secret is patience."

—Ralph Waldo Emerson

The question hung heavy in the air. As it sank, a slim flicker of hope wormed its way into the Boy.

"What if . . ." He concentrated all his attention. "What if . . ." And then it came, gushing like a geyser from the bowels of the earth.

"We'll tell her that we were hunting rabbits," the Boy began. "And I thought you were behind me. And I saw something move and I thought it was a rabbit, so I shot it. Somehow, you had gotten in front of me and so, by mistake, I shot you." The Boy, his eyes bugged out of his head, stared at this brother. "How does that sound?"

"Good," his brother responded. "Really good. My head hurts but I don't want to get in trouble."

"Say it back to me, then," the Boy ordered, gaining confidence.

"I was behind you but you didn't see me get up ahead and you believed you saw a rabbit and took a shot at it but hit me in the head instead. Is that it?"

"That's it." The Boy put his arm around his brother. "Let's rehearse it again. We have to make sure that we're saying the same, exact thing, in case they separate us."

Together, they moved through the olive orchard running the story again and again.

"That's the most moronic, idiotic maneuver I have ever heard of," the father barked. "Haven't I told you over and over never to split up when you go out with your guns? Do you not listen, or were you just trying to act like an idiot?"

"Yes, sir," the Boy stammered. "I mean, 'no, sir,' I wasn't."

Explanation of Edict IV

I'll never forget that special day when I stood in front of my condominium on Johnson Beach on Perdido Key Island in Northwest Florida. Not a cloud graced the sky, a light breeze tickled the senses, and the gentle waves of the Gulf of Mexico lapped against the shore in quiet whispers.

In sharp contrast, Ivan—a category five hurricane with sustained winds of 155 miles per hour and gusts close to 200—roared a few hundred miles away. My family and I had spent the last week glued to the Weather Channel, tracking the trajectory that saw this 500 mile–wide monster pass South of Key West and take a hard right, gather even more force in the warm waters, and, now, loom poised for a direct hit within 48 hours.

Under mandatory evacuation orders, we left.

Hours later, Ivan slammed ashore, blowing 135 miles an hour with a surge from the sea of 25 feet. In five short hours—and the worse natural disaster to ever hit Pensacola—the length of our barrier island, my condominium and the entire culture of artists, musicians, and craftspeople who had populated this corner of the earth for decades, was completely obliterated. Their low-cost housing could never be rebuilt. What took decades to develop disappeared overnight.

Recently, I walked by the empty lot where the building had once stood. The only thing left was an odd chunk of asphalt buried in sand from the parking area where I once left my car. Years of effort—gone.

Establishing a successful business always takes longer than planned, requires infinitely more energy than expected,

"After as much time as I've spent teaching you boys how to take care of your guns, how to breathe and aim and shoot properly, *and this is the way you reward me . . . with this asinine level of blatant stupidity?*"

On and on the father ranted, more concerned with his own failure as a teacher than the damage of the pellet wound. Finally, he ran out of steam.

"Take those guns and put them on the top shelf of my closet. You're both damn lucky that the pellet hit you on the forehead, the thickest bone in your body, matched only by the thickness of your brains." He shook his head.

"I have no idea what it will take for you to prove that you can be trusted enough to get your privileges restored. It'll be a miracle if you see those guns before Christmas. Get out of here—both of you."

And that was it. The Boy's insides collapsed in relief though he couldn't quite understand. No beatings. No grounding. No punishment other than taking the guns. It made no sense. He didn't get it.

And then he did.

On that day, the Boy learned the value of a lie.

and costs more money than estimated. Fifty percent of businesses started by new entrepreneurs fail in the first year, while 90 percent fail in the first three. Seldom do start-ups turn a profit before the fourth year of operation. Against these odds, a lack of understanding of the time required to succeed can mark the death of an enterprise; and signals the need for an unclouded grasp of patience.

Patience is defined as follows:

1. The will or ability to wait or endure without complaint.
2. Steadiness, endurance or perseverance in performing a task.

Notice how earlier edicts from the Code form part of the definition—*the will* stands for the decision. *To endure* speaks to commitment. *Steadiness* implies responsibility.

Performing a task comes from the conception and execution of the plan. *Patience* involves the natural process of persevering (also in the definition) for long enough to allow the accumulated actions set forth in the plan to take hold and bear fruit.

The Law of Accumulation states that if, you take the correct actions enough times, you will accomplish whatever the goal. This begs the questions: what are the "correct actions" and how many are "enough times?" Though the answer will always depend on the goal, from a perspective of patience, this does not matter. If we are determined to persist for however long it takes, we can take comfort in the fact that with every additional correct action we will get closer and that the Law of

Chapter Eight

Broken clouds dotted the late-June sky, a mosaic of grays and whites stained by intermittent pale blue.

Mid-sentence, the Old Man lifted his hand and stopped the Boy with a harshness the Boy had never heard.

"Enough," the Old Man commanded. "Your parents may have believed that rubbish but don't expect me to. What you told them was a lie and people who tell lies are liars."

The Boy felt the sting of the Old Man's words.

"I was just trying to avoid a beating," he stammered. "I would never lie to you."

"Wrong on both counts, Boy," the Old Man corrected, firm and rough. "You were trying to shirk the consequences of your actions as most humans seek to do. You thought you could get away with a story to avoid paying a price and so you lied." The Old Man turned his eyes to the water. "You are still young enough to get this right, Boy, so be still and listen."

The Old Man's fingers began their dance on the bamboo.

"Liars lie, cheaters cheat, and thieves steal," the Old Man went on. "That's what they're supposed to do. That's why they're called liars, cheats, and thieves. Human beings, unlike animals, are unique in their foolishness—their belief that they can 'beat the

Accumulation will build chits in our favor, like a success bank account that is steadily increasing. Particularly on tough days, this knowledge enables us to make one more call, draft one last proposal, stay an extra hour, and trust that these micro-steps will lead to overall success.

Complimentary to tenacious action, a patient attitude enables us to step back and evaluate more objectively, and even to periodically take a needed break to recharge, knowing that the Law of Accumulation will continue to work in our favor.

I remember a convention a while back, where toward the end of his speech, the head of an organization declared in jest: "and if you stick around long enough, any bonehead can figure out what not to do and get this right." While his commentary drew a big guffaw, there is much truth in it. When Thomas Edison was asked about failing 9,999 times on his way to inventing the lightbulb, he quickly retorted: "I didn't fail. I found out 9,999 times what didn't work so that on the 10,000 round I could figure out what did."

Indeed. As human beings, we make mistakes. In embarking on a new venture, we will make even more. Some will be the expected faux-pas associated with lack of experience; others will depend upon our own filters and backgrounds; still others may come out of left field. It doesn't matter. With patience and an open mind, in due course, we will uncover what doesn't work—and stop doing that in favor of something else. If that "something else" doesn't serve either, we will figure that out and move on to the next act. Eventually, we can't help but stumble onto a few of the "correct actions" that will move us toward success.

system' or skirt the laws of nature. A mule walks down the street and never steps into the same pothole twice. Fish know the ways of fish and birds know the ways of birds. The sockeye salmon leaves its birthplace and travels six thousand miles before returning to the exact same stream it came from to lay its eggs. The whales migrate even farther, following the same patterns year after year. In the winter, the geese fly south."

The Old Man paused. "Not sometimes or most of the time—all the time. Have you ever heard of a goose breaking away from the flock and turning north? Of course not."

A menacing cloud crept onto the horizon.

"There is a causality to all things, Boy, and nothing happens in isolation. For every cause, there is an effect, which, like the goose flying south, is never a maybe."

"What do you mean?" the Boy interrupted.

"We reap what we sow, Boy, all of us. If you study, you pass. If you don't, you fail. Simple and straightforward—even fools can see that much. The challenge lies in that most people consider the outer effect and forget the inner, sometimes far more powerful."

The Old Man drew in a long breath as if to allow the Boy a chance to catch up. "When you shot your brother, you saw the outer effect immediately. You hurt him, he started bleeding, and you left him with a mark on his forehead that he may wear his whole life." He held a beat. "The inner effect is often just as lasting."

The Old Man inhaled again. "After you hit him, did you feel afraid?" he asked.

"Yes," the Boy exclaimed immediately. "Very."

Side by side with patience stands temperance, a trusted ally that jabs us in the ribs before an outburst and helps us keep unwieldy anger in check. Its presence is critical for our success.

Imagine a vertical line with emotion at the very top and rational thought at the very bottom. The middle represents that area of balance between desire, passion, drive, ambition—the high emotional states that drive us to action—and logic, reason, systems, processes—the low rational states that craft and monitor the plan. Every time we stray too far from the balanced middle, we lose our objectivity. If we soar too high, we can fly off the handle and act impulsively without considering the consequences. If we let ourselves stray too low, we become mired in analysis and don't move to action. Both places represent danger.

However, the damage caused by paralysis happens slowly—which also means that, if recognized, it can be promptly corrected. The damage that ensues from a temper outburst, a moment of blindness, or an act of negligence that leads to the loss of ability to view a problem rationally can be permanent.

Consider the following story:

There was once a little boy who had a bad temper. His father gave him a bag of nails and told him that, every time he lost his temper, he must hammer a nail into the back of the fence behind the house. On the first day, the boy drove 37 nails into the fence. Over the next few weeks, as he learned to control his anger, the number of daily hammered nails gradually dwindled down. He discovered that it was easier to hold his temper than to drive those nails into the fence.

"Afraid of what, though?" the Old Man pushed. "Afraid that your brother had been injured or afraid of what would happen to you when your father found out?"

The Old Man glanced at the Boy.

"Don't answer," he stated. "I can see it in your eyes. You were more worried about yourself than your little brother—as most people would be . . ." the Old Man mused. "That's the inner effect, the fear that gripped you like a vise. Within that fear rests the seed for the next cause—the telling of a lie and in that lie the seed for another because on the surface it seems to work until one day you wake up to find that the harvest of all those seeds is nothing more than a crop of lies."

The Old Man's words hung in the air like the stench of a skunk or the smell of an open garbage can piled with rotting shrimp. The sky grew darker. Still, the Old Man spoke on.

"The Great Ones understand the natural laws and work within them to produce greatness." He glanced at the Boy again. "As I've suggested to you many times, let others lead small lives, not you."

The black cloud covered the last of the sun's rays and cast a shadow over the Old Man's face. Something struck his line. The Old Man jerked the pole back in one fluid motion and ignored it.

"One thing is as certain and as strict as the laws of cause and effect," he declared in a flat, monotone voice that left no room for doubt. "I will have no friend who is a liar."

Fat, sporadic drops sent the sunbathers scurrying for cover from the beach below. The Old Man sat unfazed by the rain, as steady and unyielding as the rocks below him, and said no more.

Chapter Eight   **61**

Finally, the day came when the boy didn't lose his temper at all. He told his father about it and the father suggested that, from then on, the boy pull out one nail for each day in which he held his temper. The days passed, and the young boy eventually told his father that all the nails were gone. The father took his son by the hand and led him to the fence, where he said:

"You have done well, my son, but look at the holes in the fence. The fence will never be the same. When you say things in anger, they leave a scar just like these. You can put a knife in a man and draw it out. It won't matter how many times you say 'I'm sorry'—the wound will still be there."

No one likes to be yelled at or berated and no one appreciates being put down. In the long term of a business, this approach never works. If you have a cancer in your operation or enterprise, then cut it out. Don't expect that your verbal tongue lashing or cajoling will ever fix a problem for any longer than that day or that week. It won't. You won't close a contract by yelling through a negotiation; if you do, your reputation will quickly begin to precede you and send potential partners and clients elsewhere. People, much like plants, need nurturing and caring to grow. Conversely, they will wither in the heat of criticism.

To grow an empowered and self-motivated organization, discipline yourself to hold your ire. Ask yourself, as your blood level rises: "Will I be angry about this tomorrow?" If the answer is no, then zip it. By the next day, the lesson to be imparted will remain—without the emotional charge.

Chapter Nine

The father snapped the book shut and slapped it on the dining room table.

"That's the second time in a row you got the same one wrong, Boy—your brain must be going backwards." He laughed uproariously at his own joke. "What are they teaching you in that school, anyway?" His eyes narrowed. "I heard there was some trouble over there today, some kind of a big fight. You didn't happen to be involved in that, did you?"

The Old Man's admonition flashed in the Boy's mind. He knew it would be worse on him unless he told a story. Still, the Old Man's friendship meant more to him than a whipping even though he didn't quite understand or even agree with the value of telling the truth.

"Yes, sir," he answered, his face set.

"'Yes, sir' you weren't involved or 'yes, sir' you were?" his father barked. "Talk English, Boy, not gibberish."

"Yes, sir," the Boy repeated. "A kid insulted me, so I hit him. He grabbed one of his buddies to gang up on me and I smacked him, too. Then a whole bunch of other kids jumped in."

The father stared at him, incredulous. "You mean you started the entire mess?" he demanded.

This same temperance applies to our relationship with ourselves. Acknowledging mistakes forms part of taking full responsibility. Whipping ourselves or wallowing in self-pity is an indulgent waste of time and energy—a lesson that the Old Man imparts several times to the Boy.

In *jujutsu*, if you become tense or uptight, you instantly lose 50 percent of your strength. In business, a balance must be struck between logic and reason on one side and creativity and passion on the other. The minute we err too far to either side, the equilibrium is lost, judgment goes out the window, and the enterprise suffers. Paralysis by analysis takes a while. Flying off the handle takes a second.

Guard the mind that triggers the thoughts that open the mouth. Choose your words well, if needed at all. As the old saying states: "Better a word too few, than one too many."

Patience and temperance mark the beginning of mastery over self. The Code exposes both the traits that weave themselves into the character of a Great One, as well as those that drive behavior. Patience and temperance speak more to what *not* to do—to an inner resolve of trust and restraint that forges through effort and experience. Success takes time. Those unwilling to discipline themselves to persist will never taste the holy grail. Those who prematurely rush the beachhead unfortunately get slaughtered.

Reference Chapters: 1, 4, 11, 23, 29, 35, and 36.

"No, sir," the Boy argued to no avail. "He insulted me first."

"Some kid calls you a name and you haul off and wallop him? Are you an imbecile? It's a good thing your mother can't hear this."

His father sat, shaking his head. The Boy said nothing. "I can't believe you insist on making me try to beat some sense into you. Go on," he ordered, "you know what to do."

The Boy rose from the table, walked to the master bedroom, ignored his mother wheezing in the bed, and pulled the belt from the drawer. In silence, he returned to the dining room, placed the belt on the tablecloth, and stripped off his shirt. Resolute, he gripped the back of his own chair and waited.

"Whack," came the belt. The Boy flinched without a sound.

"Whack," struck the second blow. Again, the Boy suppressed his visceral desire to scream. "Not this time," the Boy vowed to himself. "This time, I don't cry."

"Don't you know that it hurts me more than it hurts you to have to hit you like this?" his father clamored. He raised his arm high.

"Whack."

The belt bit into the muscle above the Boy's tail bone. His knuckles turned white on the chair as he clamped his jaw shut to stop his lips from quivering.

"Not a chance," the Boy willed, ignoring the searing cuts from the rough leather.

"Whack."

His father pulled his wrist back. "What's it going to take to get you to understand that it hurts less to stay out of trouble than to feel my belt on your back?"

V. *Thou shall act with courage.*

"Courage is the most important of all virtues, because without it we can't practice any other virtue with consistency."

—Maya Angelou

Again and again, his father whipped him, growing more and more angry with each blow the Boy withstood without a yelp.

"Whack—whack—whack."

The leather strip ripped through the Boy's flesh. He uttered not a peep, engaged in a desperate, savage fight to keep his mouth locked shut.

The Boy matched his father's fury with his own inner rage, held his teeth clenched, forced the tears back, and endured the worse beating of his life.

Eventually, his father lost the will to continue, threw the belt on the floor, and collapsed in his chair.

"Put it away," he spat at the Boy.

In complete silence the Boy rejected the burn from the open welts as he reached down to pick up the belt. He returned it to the chest of drawers without even a glance at his mother and retired to his room. Flat on his bed, he could no longer hold anything in. The floodgates burst open. He cried hard, bitter tears until he soaked his pillowcase through.

Exhausted, he fell asleep with one burning resolve.

"I beat him once," he swore to himself. "I will beat him again."

Explanation of Edict V

At age 17, I broke my leg in the final game of the varsity soccer season—a complex fracture that required a full-length leg cast from hip to toe, elevated by ropes and pulleys for the first full month following the break. As I lay in bed one night in my room at the far end of my father's rambling ranch-style house, I heard some noise outside. In an instant I realized that burglars were attempting to break in through the kitchen below me. Because of my leg, I could not run for help. I attempted to scream only to find that my vocal chords froze in fear. I couldn't escape, couldn't yell, and couldn't move as I listened to the would-be criminals work on jimmying the window in the downstairs breakfast alcove.

In utter terror, I was completely paralyzed.

On a recent family ski trip, my 9-year-old son Linus began boasting after five days on the snow that he could ski an expert, double-diamond slope—a claim that, much to the rest of our crew's chagrin, magnified as time went on. Despite my paternal reservations, I felt confident that I could get him down the mountain safely. As a father, I sensed that a valuable lesson might be in the making; and in the early afternoon on day six, off we went to the top of the mountain. After some fairly aggressive terrain near the peak, we crested over the ridge and onto the very steep down-grade called Geronimo.

"C'mon," I urged, and took a couple of turns.

When I turned to glance up, the only thing moving on Linus were his quivering lips and the tears that dripped

Chapter Ten

The Boy scrambled up the rocks in a state of turmoil.

"See what telling the truth got me," he spewed at the Old Man as he pulled up his shirt and spun around. The welts and bruises blended with the newly formed scabs in broken lines like railroad tracks in an abandoned, rusted yard. The Old Man opened his knife, reached into his bag for the aloe, and gently placed long slivers of the guts of the leaf on the blisters and fledgling crusts.

"You'll have to be still in the open air so the plant can do its work," he said simply. With soft hands he anointed the bloody skin.

Side by side they sat and for a long while they watched the seagulls frolic in the easy surf, bobbing up and down on the waves like corks on the open sea.

"I remember the first time I told a lie," the Old Man began.

"I had taken some chocolate from the kitchen cabinet and blamed it on my sister who was a year younger. She denied everything and I guess I should have checked in a mirror because I never saw the tiny brown stain on my collar. My father listened to me, got up, and left the house after telling me to stay put. About fifteen minutes later he came back with a bag full of huge chocolate

down his cheeks. I stepped back up the slope, gave him a hug, and stooped down to the level of his eyes.

"I'm really scared, Dad," he mumbled.

"I know, son," I answered. "It's okay. You can do this. I'll help you."

It became quickly apparent that all he had learned in the previous five days had flown out the window of his memory. He stood frozen as a statue and could only be coaxed to move forward with tiny baby steps. In a slow and deliberate fashion we slinked our way down the mountain. The braggart nature died a rapid demise somewhere on the hill.

In both of these situations—one that took place over 30 years ago, and another just this past year—Linus and I became utterly helpless in the face of fear. All logic and reason disappeared. Our ability to cope vanished. The world, in essence, shut down and caved in around us.

In business, fear lurks as enemy number one—a foe that often sneaks through the cracks in our armor in insidious and parasitic ways. Take the big-thinking visionary who bursts with big ideas, innovations, and new products. Beneath the blustery surface sits a boy that didn't do so well in math, hates numbers and details, and has difficulty staying on task. As a consequence, the company flounders in a sea of red ink, with lots of activity and a concept-of-the-week to fix the "problem" of poor cash management.

Take the number-crunching accountant entrepreneur who closely tabulates every dollar, carefully watches the pennies, yet loathes change, and—with no lack of work ethic—sharpens his pencil with every decrease in the margins, only to realize that what used to work no longer

bars of all kinds—white, milk, dark, mixed. He stepped in the pantry and pulled out a mop and a bucket. 'Son,' he said, 'If chocolate is so important to you that you have to lie about it, then I guess you must really need some. I picked up a few different types and you're going to finish every last one!' With that, he dumped the chocolates in the bucket and returned to reading the newspaper."

The Old Man paused in reflection. "The first bar tasted good, I think . . . and maybe the second. With 10 or 12 bars to go, I realized what the bucket was for. It got to the point where I threw up every one I choked down. My father rested calmly on the couch the whole time, unaffected. I knew better than to cross him, though it was not his style to hit anyone. He dreamt up other ways of making a lesson stick. I vomited chocolate until I could barely eat more than a small square at a time. To this day, I can't stand the stuff. That's why I carry the *menta*."

The Boy started to chuckle. The more he thought about it the harder he laughed and the Old Man roared with him.

"I guess he showed you," the Boy jested before bursting out laughing again.

"In a way that I've never forgotten," the Old Man concluded, "though the lesson took a while longer to take hold. At first I only thought about hating chocolate. Later, I understood about consequences."

The Boy put his chin in his hands and stared at the foam on the swells. Particles of straw-colored seaweed drifted lazily by. "I guess I shouldn't have decked that kid at school," he admitted.

The Old Man plucked once on his fishing line.

"When people hurt others," he shared, "usually it means that they don't like themselves—that they have to prove themselves

does. It's the same way that 8-tracks gave way to cassettes, which in turn yielded to compact discs that now are downloaded from the internet directly onto a hand-held PDA or iPod that didn't even exist a few years back.

In both cases, the fear of confronting the unknown and not seeking an alternative outside of one's personal comfort zone will lead to a resounding failure. The challenge lies in the mind. We must recognize our own shortcomings and make up for them in some way. What if the big-thinker hooked up with the number-cruncher and found a way to collaborate despite their differences—and celebrated their strengths? Together, they might build a great enterprise.

Does this seem like a BGO (Blinding Glimpse of the Obvious)? Sure, from the outside, much like the Monday morning quarterback, anyone can give advice. Why didn't the big-thinker hire a number-cruncher in the first place? The answer will soon become clear.

Many people equate courage with the absence of fear. Not so at all. Even highly courageous individuals will, from time to time, face various types of fear. The obvious fears of death and bodily harm top a long list of other incarnations that, especially in business, can greatly damage an enterprise. What about the subordinate who never speaks for fear of repercussion? What about the boss who can't delegate for fear that he'll lose control? What about the accountant who simply crunches numbers and fails to point out negative trends for fear of being labeled unpopular or made into a scapegoat? What about the small business owner or sales executive who won't follow up on old and prospective accounts for fear of rejection?

superior because they actually feel 'less than' or not worthy." The Old Man's finger moved from the line to the pole.

"Sometimes," he said, "for the same reason, people hurt themselves—a classic sign of low self-esteem. 'I don't like me so therefore I'll hurt me and at least that way I'll gain some attention.' Most people never figure out that happiness is an inside job and that the only person you can truly be in charge of is you. You always know when you've told the truth or lied. To be honest is a matter of honor and I, for one, am proud of you."

The Old Man's last three words filled the space around the Boy with a warm glow, like a hot shower in the winter or the first sip of steaming cocoa.

"Proud of you." No one had ever said that to him. The words turned the air's taste sweet, the breeze cool and refreshing. He basked in the newness of an unfamiliar feeling and decided that he liked it. A smile danced across his lips.

"Yes," he affirmed. "Proud of me."

He liked it a lot.

Courage stands for the ability to confront and handle that fear—whatever it may be and wherever it may come from. In the dictionary, *courage* is defined as "the attitude or response of facing and dealing with anything recognized as dangerous, difficult, or painful."

Notice that there's no mention of avoidance, escape, circumvention, or denial in the definition.

The way of a Great One involves a continuous internal battle against a variety of factors—the blindness that keeps our perception cloudy; the immense creativity within each of us that can drive us off task; the desire to act before thinking instead of thinking first and then acting; the charge forward, damn-the-torpedoes nature that keeps us mired in a whirlwind of activity from which we awaken (or not) surrounded by the ashes of what we sought to build.

This is an active, ongoing struggle that requires courage. And, in this process, our best friend is *repetition*.

Repetition leads to competence. Competence breeds confidence. Confidence overcomes fear and leads to courage—the courage to face whatever comes next.

Let me share a secret. Ever since that helpless night with my leg in traction (which fortunately ended without incident), I have lived with the fear that I might be attacked or assaulted and will once again freeze and suffer all the repercussions that one can conjure—harm to loved ones, rape, injury, you name it. It is not something that I have been able to will away—despite therapy, hypnosis, spiritual practices, or other treatment. It is very real to me, regardless of the fact that we no longer live in the

Chapter Eleven

The Boy left the house angry—angry at his father, at the world in general, but mostly at himself for being dumb enough to actually buy that his father would let him go to the game.

He remembered the moment when he asked for permission over breakfast.

"Sure," his father said, and his hopes soared only to be dashed by the tagline, ". . . if you finish varnishing the beams in the dining room first."

"That's impossible," the Boy blurted. His father shrugged with a smug look.

"What a jerk," the Boy thought, more directed at himself than his father. "I can't believe I am so stupid and gullible."

Still, the Boy gave it his best shot, hoping that maybe, just maybe, if he worked as hard as he could, he'd knock it out on time.

Fueled by fury, he sanded down the wood as fast as his arms would move. Beam after beam, with sweat dripping down his back, he labored on until his palms rubbed almost raw.

By early afternoon, he knew it was futile. As the hours ticked away, he completed the job, seething with bitterness and disappointment that grew inside him like a tumor. He applied the last

sink-or-swim, draw-your-revolver, and kill-or-be-killed world that forged strong men and women out of sheer survival. Today, we must find other methods.

To overcome this fear, I drive the better part of an hour to *jujutsu*, where I know before each class starts that I will have to mentally confront my fear of bodily harm. It's a running joke among my fellow practitioners that we pay good money to show up, sweat, and get beat upon relentlessly, class after class. Why? Because I know that, if I keep showing up, one day the relentless repetition will turn into competence, which will in turn lead to confidence and continue to build the courage to square off against ever-greater adversaries. I yearn for that result, and I demand it of myself. Therefore, I show up, confront the fear, and do the exercises over and over until I master them.

Consider the salesman on his first call. He fumbles through a mostly forgotten script, survives the experience, and goes back to his car for another cup of coffee and a chance to regroup. On the second call, he at least has the experience of having survived the first one. He lucks out on number five and makes a sale. More than confidence, he feels a sense of relief—at least it's possible . . .

In the first month, he hits one out of ten. While some might be discouraged, others keep knocking. Pay attention, as this is a key point—*anyone* can knock. *Only a few do—those who muster up the courage.*

By month three, he's up to two out of ten. By month six, he closes three out of ten. Now he is making a living.

stroke, threw the brush into a bucket of paint thinner, and slipped out the front door.

He ambled down the road toward the stadium kicking rocks as hard as he could at nothing in particular. He decided to slip through the forbidden orchard, the one he'd been ordered to stay out of, and take a short cut. No one could see him anyway, he rationalized. Everyone else was at the game.

He crossed the neatly tilled rows to the apricot tree in the center and began to climb, knowing that he could see down onto the soccer pitch from the top.

Boiling with rage, he poked his head through the canopy in time to watch the fans storm the field in celebration.

"We won," he sputtered, "and I missed it all," he added as he smashed his fist into the tree.

At the apex of his own self-loathing, he shifted his weight and stepped onto a branch that couldn't hold him.

It snapped. He tumbled through the tree, grasping wildly at leaves that came off in his hands, until he hit the ground with a dull thud.

In blinding pain, he turned slowly to discover his elbow bent back in an inverted V—misshapen and grotesque like a raw chicken wing after the bone is snapped.

Through the agony, in disbelief, he stared at his own broken arm.

Repetition, repetition, repetition. By the end of the first year, he averages a 40 percent close rate. By the end of the second year, he plateaus at 50 percent and suddenly realizes that his family will never starve. Who knows how far he will go if he keeps working on his craft.

Fear—a natural state once needed for survival and protection from danger—also paralyzes and demoralizes. And, while it does not *erase* fear, courage enables us to confront it and move forward. Once in action, repetition turns the difficult into easy and the "fear-full" into "fear-less"—never wiping out all fear, but making it less important and less likely to immobilize us.

Courage—much like patience, temperance, responsibility, and decision making—originates in the mind and they all work in unison. The Code paints the image of a Great One who embraces these mental traits and, through years of repeated application, works with them effortlessly.

One by one, the Old Man exposes these to the Boy with the invitation to try each of them.

On a side note, in French, the word *coeur* means *heart*. Quite appropriately, "cour-age" might also be deemed the "age of the heart."

Reference Chapter: 2, 17, 22, 26, 32, 36, and Epilogue.

Book 2

The Battle

"Since then, at an uncertain hour,

That agony returns;

And till my ghastly tale is told,

This heart within me burns."

—Samuel Taylor Coleridge
(*The Rime of the Ancient Mariner*)

VI. *Thou shall cultivate passion.*

"There is no passion like that of a functionary for his function."

—Georges Clemenceau

Chapter Twelve

"I got kicked out of school," the Boy blurted out without a hello.

The Old Man nodded.

"One of the *chulos* made fun of my cast, so I hit him with it." The Boy paused. "I guess I broke his tooth."

"I heard," the Old Man responded. "News travels fast around here—as you know." He adjusted his fishing pole with his foot.

"I got kicked out of school, too, Boy," the Old Man added. "By the bombers." He drew in a loud breath. "We all did."

"What do you mean?" the Boy asked.

The Old man glanced at him and smiled. "When the Great War started, no one believed it would reach us. For months we did nothing except listen to the radio for reports. Then one day the planes came and the bombs fell. One of them hit our school. We couldn't go back for over two years."

"What did you do?"

"We moved into the hills and dug underground caves far enough away that we didn't matter to the soldiers. A lot of families did. During the daytime we stayed out of sight and never saw anyone." The Old Man's eyes turned distant.

"How did you eat?" the Boy pestered.

The Old Man rubbed his forehead as if to ease a painful memory. "At night we picked fruit from the orchards—and green

Explanation of Edict VI

Of the many dictionary definitions for *passion*, one stands out above the others: "extreme, compelling emotion; intense emotional drive or excitement . . ."

Lust, desire, craving, yearning, and many other terms attempt to explain the necessary passion for success that in essence stands for "wanting" it, at whatever price wanting that success will extract.

As young children, we place ourselves with reckless abandon anywhere we want to be, without restrictions. A child that wants to drive a Formula-1 car makes race tracks with his spaghetti and sees him or herself victoriously speeding around. We build castles in the sand as glorious as Buckingham Palace or Versailles and take reign of them as the knight in shining armor, the fair maiden, king, or queen. We view ourselves clearly as the leading man or lady on a giant silver screen and never doubt that eventuality.

Then the realists and the naysayers set in, and our childhood promises and fantasies die a gradual death—replaced, more often than not, by excuses. Adults become so conditioned to seeing things in the physical realm that we forget the source of uninhibited pure and free creation—the mind.

"Get a real job."

"There's no time for that now."

almonds. We set traps that gave us an occasional rabbit. We had a goat that produced a little milk. It was very hard."

"Why didn't you fight?" the Boy insisted.

"Many people did and many people died," the Old Man admitted with bitterness. "My older brother and my cousin went to the front. Both were killed." He spat into the water. "I learned the hard way that violence never yields anything good. There are other, better ways to fight."

"I'm sorry," the Boy stated quietly.

"It is difficult to build and easy to destroy," the Old Man maintained. "It is easy to break things or hurt people and the person that does so feels a certain sense of false power as if that makes them stronger. It doesn't. All it does is leave a gaping hole inside that is tough to fill and tougher to heal. Some of the effects are immediate, like being kicked out of school. Others take longer and can linger for years, like the stigma caused by your actions and the shame that goes with it. The universe is unyielding in its strictness. Everyone must pay."

The Boy opened his mouth to speak but the Old Man's upheld hand caused him to stop.

"Still," he concluded, "anyone can decide at anytime to change their ways. It just gets harder the longer you wait."

"How do you mean, Old Man?" the Boy questioned.

"When a fire burns a forest to the ground, does nature wait to clear away the debris before birthing new plants?" the Old Man queried rhetorically. "Of course not. Green shoots sprout from the ashes and around the blackened tree trunks."

He placed his palm on the Boy's shoulder. "So it is with you. You can decide right now to use your mind and step out of the darkness. The land never asks for your intentions or aspirations. It

"You need to get serious."

"Stop dreaming."

What so many fail to understand is that, to endure the arduous, difficult journey to success, we all need that "compelling emotion" to keep us going through the rough spots, the challenges, and the setbacks.

In the wake of the Great Depression, hotelier Conrad Hilton faced bankruptcy and the total collapse of his hotel chain. Instead of despairing, he cut out a picture of the Waldorf Astoria in all its splendor and pasted it on to his desk so that every day he gazed upon it and fueled his passion. Not only did he recover his empire, less than 20 years later he actually bought the Waldorf.

Abraham Lincoln failed time after time at virtually everything he tried. Born into poverty, Lincoln lost eight elections, failed twice in business, and suffered a nervous breakdown that kept him bedridden for six months. Yet his desire was so strong that it drove him to such a level that he ended up in the White House—and became one of the most revered presidents in history.

A good friend of mine named Ruben Gonzalez grew up with a dream to be an Olympic athlete. Much to his chagrin, he had minimal athletic ability and little more than his own desire to help his quest. He researched the most difficult sports in the games—those with the greatest athlete attrition—and discovered the luge, a pursuit

just wants seeds. If you plant many, you will have a big crop. If you don't, you starve. If you plant many but don't water them or pull the weeds, you will have a poor crop. If you do, you reap a rich one. Life is like that. If you allow the seeds of violence to grow, they will consume you. You will fall into the very hole that you create within yourself, from which there is seldom any escape."

The Old Man turned to the Boy. "Are you switching to the village school?"

"Yes," the Boy responded. "*Mañana.*"

"You have a chance for a fresh start," the Old Man admonished. "I wonder what you'll do with it."

The Boy wondered if the Old Man could really understand, though he understood most things. Tomorrow, once again, he would be the outcast, the new kid—and everyone would know why he was there.

"They'll pick on me even more if they think I'm a wimp," the Boy argued.

"If you let them get to you and respond to their taunts, then they control you, and they win. You give up all of your power." The Old Man refused to back down. "If you use your mind to control your emotions and don't react, you win. It's that simple. Life is a constant battle between darkness and light. Whenever there is light, darkness disappears. If darkness creeps in, it eclipses the light. It is always easier to fall into the dark. You don't even have to do anything and our natural tendencies will take us there. It takes effort, perseverance, and constant vigilance to choose to step into the light. That's what the Great Ones do." The Old Man held a beat. "The rest—as we've discussed many times—are sleepwalkers."

that left athlete's bodies littered on the track, with broken bones and broken spirits. Having been born in Houston, Texas, Ruben had never even seen snow. Undeterred by this fact, he hung a poster of a luge man above his bed where he could wake up in the morning and go to sleep every night with his first and last thoughts firmly fixed on making the Olympics. Today, Ruben travels the world as a motivational speaker sharing his message of desire and perseverance—when he's not in some frigid climate training for his Fourth Olympiad.

In the interviews for *Modest to Millions*, the same message came through loud and clear: "The guys that are the most successful are the ones that just want it more," said one industry giant. "I'll take staying power over brain power any day of the week," quoted another, again referencing that driving desire to stick it out for however long it takes in order to succeed.

Studies repeatedly prove that productivity goes up for those who take a day off each week, a weekend off every month, and a long vacation each year. They point to the need for rest and rejuvenation, though I believe they overlook another crucial aspect. In down time and in stillness, we have a chance to dream again— to birth a new idea, to come up with a better way of accomplishing a goal, to allow an innovation to bubble out. Dreams, like the muscles in our bodies and the skin on our faces, fade without exercise. We

The deep burnt orange ball hung in the sky as if suspended by a thread. The Boy sat and watched without interest as the Old Man battled a fish that eventually got away. He pondered the Old Man's words, wondering what the dawn would bring and praying, as he often did, that the sun would stop moving and their day together would never end.

He tapped his cast on the rocks by the Old Man's leg and stared into the waves.

pigeonhole ourselves into tiny boxes with defined walls. We isolate into cocoons that never turn into butterflies; and, day by day, we deepen the mud levels that keep us prisoners. We lose our edge, and we let our blades dim from razor sharp to butter soft.

We must therefore take an *active* role in fueling the passion that keeps us churning and moving toward our goals. We have to focus on our goals and dreams, visualize them in full living color. What do you see? What do you feel? What do you smell? What are the shapes and textures around you? What does your office look like in your accomplished company? What suit will you wear to accept the award for "fastest growing company" in your sector or the plaque for the philanthropic donation that you made from your profits?

So put up a dream board; fill a box full of pictures of the things you will acquire; tape a photograph of something you want on your bathroom mirror; do anything that reminds you of why you work so hard.

Talk to yourself in the present affirmative. Feed the subconscious with positive imagery that paints your picture of success.

From beginning to end in the story, the Old Man helps the Boy awaken to the dream of becoming a Great One, of refusing to settle, of playing big and never sleepwalking. He fuels that desire in the Boy, much in the way that we must all fuel that desire for ourselves.

Chapter Thirteen

His royal highness spoke from his perch at the head of the dining room table.

"How was your first day of school?" he demanded.

"Good, I guess," the Boy responded. "Sir," he added.

"What do you mean, you 'guess'? It either was or it wasn't, Boy. Stop being so wishy-washy." The father paused for a bite. "What did you learn?"

"History, sir," the Boy answered. "About Spanish royalty, the kings and queens of Europe. Sir."

"I bet you wanted to be one, too, didn't you Boy," he chuckled between mouthfuls. "King of the local varnishers—that would be you." He set down his fork, suddenly serious. "Did you get in any fights?"

"No, sir," the Boy exclaimed, though he remembered in vivid detail how close he came.

The class tough guy made a comment about his cast and baseball, how the Boy could play and didn't even need a real bat. On sheer impulse the Boy cocked his arm back as if to tee off on him. At the last second, the Old Man's words flashed through his mind: "You give up all your power. You lose."

Somehow the Boy held back, forced a sneer, and said: "You wanna' be the ball?" half-taunting, half-joking.

At the end of their lives, most people leave no record of their passing other than the few hundred thousand dollars of products and services consumed over the course of their existence. The Great Ones find a reason for fully living, for striving and pushing to new heights. As part of that Code, we *must cultivate passion*.

Reference Chapters: 10, 15, 17, 35, and 38.

The bully laughed and the Boy laughed with him. Just like that, he made a friend and was instantly known as someone not to push around. He noticed how much better that felt.

"I'm leaving tomorrow," his father declared. "I'll be gone through next Monday."

The words took a moment to sink. The Boy suppressed the surge of glee that coursed through him like an electric current. He kept his eyes on his plate.

"Oh?" the Boy questioned. "Where are you going? Who's going to take care of Mom?"

"The neighbor will stop by every day," his father explained. "I'm going to England on business."

"Yeah, right," the Boy thought to himself.

"If you behave yourselves, I might bring you something," his father taunted, true to form. "What do you want?"

The Boy chose his words carefully. To say the wrong thing might ruin his chances.

"We could use a new game," he said. "Something a bit more complicated."

The Boy's only joy with his father came in playing games—because he could beat him. A familiar pattern held each time. His father would buy a game and, in the beginning, his father would win. Within a few months, the Boy would figure the game out and the fortunes would turn. As soon as his father began to lose, he stopped playing.

The only exception was chess. Every fortnight or so his father would challenge him. The Boy played without mercy, every fiber in his being intent on one purpose—to win—no, to crush him like a palmetto bug on the sidewalk. His father had little chance.

VII. *Thou shall exercise discipline.*

Watch your thoughts; they become words.
Watch your words; they become actions.
Watch your actions; they become habits.
Watch your habits; they become character.
Watch your character; it becomes your destiny.

—Unknown

Sometimes the Boy walked to the town square and took on the men who brought their chess boards most afternoons.

He beat them, too.

"I'll see what I can find." His father's words snapped him back to reality. "Now clear the table and get to your homework."

The Boy leapt from his chair and turned into the kitchen, where he could no longer suppress his delight. A grin lit up his face from ear to ear.

"A week of peace without him," he voiced internally. "Pure paradise."

He picked up a brush and began to scrub. He glanced at his little brother as he handed him the clean, dripping plates.

Together they wiped and smiled.

Explanation for Edict VII

Discipline: the willingness to stay on task, avoid distractions, and do what must be done regardless of the circumstances. Those who understand the absolute requirement of disciplined thought and action do what they need to do, regardless of whether they feel like it or not, are in the mood or not, have a hangover or a cold, it rains, shines, or otherwise.

In a world replete with wasted talent, an average disciplined individual will win out over an undisciplined superstar every time. As best-selling author, H. Jackson Brown, once said: "Talent without discipline is like an octopus on roller skates. There is a whole lot of movement—you just don't know if you're moving forward, backwards, or sideways."

Discipline means that you get up and make the phone calls. You cross the is and dot the ts. You do today what others won't do to have tomorrow what others only dream about.

The enemy of discipline is entitlement. The entitled person believes that, because of their birthright, ethnicity, last name, socio-economic upbringing, or any other outside factor, they should be given more than they rightfully earn. They expect handouts and look to assign blame or circumstances on others when plans don't go their way. They seldom take responsibility, and they avoid accountability all together.

Chapter Fourteen

The Boy ambled down the road away from his house content and at ease. He climbed the wall into the olive orchard and stood in the neatly tilled dirt that extended in triangular rows for the length of the field. He stepped on the peaks and sank to his ankles, an odd sense of power that caused him to walk all the way to the other side, crunching with every step.

He left a zippered trail in his wake as he moved onto the foothills that skirted his favorite mountain.

The birds chattered above. A brown and gray rabbit darted from brush to brush. A lazy flock of sheep meandered along the gentle incline that led up to the base, followed by a shepherd who waved a hand in greeting.

The Boy waved back.

Without hurry, his mountain boots carried him toward the summit. He stopped to check beneath the bramble bushes for wild asparagus, the long, ultra-thin stalks that snapped at the base and tasted so good in *tortilla Española*—even better than the original recipe.

He collected a handful by the time he reached the top, where he paused to greet the only monument he ever cared about.

The ten by ten concrete base rose out of the ground like a giant helicopter pad. The pile of rocks squatted atop the cement in

Discipline counters this foe directly. If you do the work, you get paid. If you don't, you starve. Put your pants on one leg at a time like the rest of the world and hit the pavement, one step in front of the other. Prospect, and you will make sales. Don't prospect, and you won't. Prospect extra, and you will make more sales. Continue—and you will set records.

Disciplined people do first things first while the scattered majority follows their whims.

Writers must write.

Singers must sing.

Salesmen must sell.

Business owners must network.

And all of the above, to maximize their success, must do their core activities in a disciplined way, using disciplined thinking.

Disciplined thinking means that you assess the risks and rewards that accompany an activity; and, in a methodical, deliberate fashion, determine which of those risks are under your control and which are not. Instead of acting in any type of brash way, it requests that you then figure out which of those risks can be brought from out of to under your control or at least be influenced in your favor. Then—and only then—does the disciplined thinker *act*.

Note that patience and temperance assist the disciplined thinker, as does a properly conceived plan. Too

the shape of a pyramid without a tip, and anchored in its peak stood a massive wooden cross, proud and erect, that scratched a hundred feet into the sky and could be seen for 20 kilometers in any direction.

The Boy glanced up, as he always did, and stood in reverence before sitting on the concrete with his back to the rocks.

He questioned whether it was sacrilegious to do so, or perhaps a sin, though he did not consider himself particularly reverent. He went to church with most of the other boys, listened to the messages of hope, and discarded those overly guilt-laden diatribes that made no sense to him given his current lot. He liked the young priest who stooped down to shake his hand, carried the *menta* in his pocket like the Old Man, and passed it out to all the kids in the square after the services while they played marbles.

He reached into his pocket and stroked his emerald tiger's eye shooter for good luck.

The Boy's gaze fell into the infinite Mediterranean that sprawled in all directions beyond the horizon—a fluid blanket that never rested, never tired, and, in some almost magical way, gave him strength. His eyes looked without seeing, his mind far, far away in a place of more questions than answers, more confusion than clarity, where demons and voices shouted, cackled, whispered, and vied for attention in myriad moving pictures that swirled and made his head hurt.

He flashed on his new friend, the bully, and wondered if this budding alliance would prove good or bad.

He heard the ring of the Old Man's words—"Lead a big life"—and wondered what that meant, if he could do it or if he wanted to.

often, new business owners, in particular, confuse activity with productivity. Activity alone makes you tired; productivity gets you paid. The disciplined thinker understands that, prior to charging out the door to make sales, the way to success starts with preparation, due diligence, identifying the customers' needs, and finding ways to meet them. Discipline also involves sticking to the plan, executing it, and evaluating the results afterward—not changing direction mid-stream.

All great teams take disciplined action toward their goals. Other teams, often with far more talent, may win a few games until the lack of discipline catches up with them and they fall.

In business, a failure to exercise discipline is the kiss of death. Without discipline, activity cannot be measured. Without measured activity, the source of positive results cannot be tracked. Without tracking, company personnel run all over the place in different directions. No one can point to the successful actions that bear repeating. Some take undeserved credit; others circle aimlessly without producing. The ensuing chaos will bring any operation down.

Discipline equals and demands accountability—to oneself, the team, and the company goals. What is your part and are you playing it? How are you keeping track? What else could you add? There are three is in the word *discipline*—the same number as in the word *responsibility*. Both traits depend solely on you.

He thought about "the Great Ones" and asked himself what that would be like, what did they do, could he, the Boy, ever . . .

He picked up an asparagus stalk and tied it into a knot, a trifle to keep his fingers busy as for a moment, a brief moment, he allowed himself to dream.

Could it even be possible?

The asparagus yellowed in the afternoon sun. The shadows lengthened, the breeze stirred, a brown chameleon basked on the rock next to the Boy's foot. His eyelids fluttered and shut, blocking out the world, the pain, and the questions. For a time his peace continued and he rested, and the next day was Sunday, his favorite day.

The Great Ones embrace discipline as a friend and ally, and watch their thoughts, words, and actions with great care. As Aristotle once professed: "We are what we repeatedly do. Excellence is not an act, but a habit."

Reference Chapters: 16, 19, 20, 23, 28, and 34.

Chapter Fifteen

"He'll be back tomorrow," the Boy spewed, tossing his words into the air.

The Old Man said nothing.

"It's been so nice around here without him," the Boy vented. "I know this may sound terrible but in some ways I wish he had a car accident or something."

The Old Man rested in serene silence, his ancient palm lightly cupped around the bamboo pole.

"I don't know why you continue to give your power away," the Old Man responded, finally. "He's not even here and you let him control your thoughts as if you want to invite a challenge that doesn't exist yet. That makes no sense."

The Old Man tugged lightly on his line. "I understand your wish to be left alone. Still, he is your father, those are your cards, and that is the hand you have to play—unless you want him to play it for you."

The Boy hated it when the Old Man chastised him, even though, on some level, he knew that the Old Man meant well. It made him feel small and reminded him that he all too often disappointed the Old Man—which he hated even more. Only the Old Man could reach him this way, where he could hear the message without becoming so defensive that his walls blocked it

VIII. *Thou shall remain single-minded.*

"All happiness depends on courage and work. I have had many periods of wretchedness, but with energy and above all with illusions, I pulled through them all".

—Honore de Balzac

out. Only because he felt how much the Old Man cared could he even listen.

A lone tear of frustration escaped from the corner of his eye and rolled halfway down his cheek before he wiped it away with his wrist.

"Look at the birds and the waves and the clouds and the sun," the Old Man urged. "Look at the people playing ball with their paddles and the infants that sit naked in the foam that laps around them, slapping it with their tiny hands. There is so much joy if you will only seek it out." The Old Man paused. "I keep telling you, Boy, master your mind. Step into the light. It's right there in front of you."

The Boy's face grew sullen. He stared at his toes trapped in his dark sandals, crowned by a line of brown around the edges from the dust on the dirt path. At least they were broken in, he thought.

Suddenly, a forgotten image flashed before him. He broke into a grin and turned to the Old Man. "I got the boat," he stated.

"Really?" The Old Man sounded surprised. "The 350?"

"Yup," the Boy chirped. "It's already at the '*Club Maritimo*.' You can't see it because it's hidden by the 420s and 470s."

"What color?" the Old Man asked.

"Deep red with white sails, just like I pictured," the Boy responded in a satisfied tone. "I got it for my birthday, last Wednesday—from my grandmother." The Boy glanced at the Old Man. "You didn't think *he* would give it to me, did you?" he tacked on with a sneer.

The Old Man began to speak. The Boy interrupted him. "I know, I know, focus on the positive." The Boy grinned again. "Two more lessons and I can go out on my own. My instructor already promised."

Explanation of Edict VIII

My father's seeing eye dog's final test took place on the streets of Manhattan. With ease, Nashua guided my father through the foot traffic, across the busy cross walks, and along the sidewalk for many blocks.

Sheep dogs in New Zealand frolic across the hills with boundless joy, able to manage several hundred sheep without a hitch, where a mere bark can bunch, organize, and move an entire flock.

Guard dogs everywhere remain so focused that nothing escapes their keen smell, alert ears, and laser sharp eyes. An intrusion is detected within seconds and rapidly dealt with.

These highly successful dogs share a common trait: the ability to remain single-minded.

Regrettably, human beings do not possess this trait; they get distracted by almost anything, at almost any time. The advent of video and other high-tech gadgetry has done nothing but shorten our attention span, with manufacturers competing to hold our interest through myriad effects and other distracters that supposedly "captivate" us. The number of craftspeople continues to dwindle as fewer and fewer artisans can sit still for long enough to carve a wooden object, weave reeds, or mold clay. While some may argue that technological advancements have made certain professions obsolete, the price in human capital has been steep.

"That's good," the Old Man asserted. "It will give you some independence and a sense of freedom that you must always respect and never take for granted." The Old Man switched hands on his pole. "There are many who have far less freedom than you though, in the end, true freedom lies in the mind."

"I can't wait," the Boy stated, somewhat smug. "Freedom to get away from him."

The Old Man ignored the remark.

"Now you see the value of hard work," the Old Man acknowledged. "If you hadn't passed all your courses, you couldn't go out. What good is a sailboat without a sailor?"

The Old Man put his right hand on the Boy's left shoulder. "You earned every certification yourself. I'm proud of you."

Those words again.

The Boy beamed and for a moment it was as if the world stood still, as if a bubble surrounded the two of them in a place all their own—a place where emotion stopped time and nothing mattered but that feeling of worthiness, so unfamiliar and new. The Boy basked in the stillness until the Old Man reached into his bag and removed a package wrapped in the pale waxed paper from the local market.

"Happy Birthday," the Old Man declared. "You didn't think I'd forget, did you?" he tacked on with a hint of mischief. "Go ahead. Open it."

The Boy ripped off the paper and held an old leather-bound volume in his hand. The cover read *The Count of Montecristo*.

"It's a book," the Boy uttered, a tad confused.

"By Dumas, one of the Great Ones," the Old Man affirmed. "About one of the Great Ones," he added.

"What's a 'Count'?" the Boy queried.

Today, very few have the stick-to-itiveness to stay after practice and kick a ball against a wall for an extra hour, or shoot another 100 free throws on the basketball court, or catch a baseball until the light makes it impossible to see. We seldom walk through forests to learn how to track an animal, blow a duck call a thousand times until it sounds like the real thing, or spend 45 minutes mixing paint until we create the perfect shade for our canvas. We want right-now results: powders that build muscle; pills that melt fat; point-and-click templates that save us from thinking on our own.

Unfortunately, this growing inability to stay on task will never lead to greatness.

Consider this as you look back over the Code. First, we make a decision. Then we conceive a plan. We take responsibility for that plan and begin to execute on it. We patiently yet courageously take disciplined action while cultivating passion for the achievement of our goal.

What's left? To *stay on it*. Refuse to fall off task. Refocus again and again. Push away those who pull on you. Shut them out. Build a mental wall of protection against noise, gossip, chatter, and junk. Stop repeatedly checking your e-mail. Turn your cell phone or your PDA off. Make the decision to stick with your plan and don't deviate.

Studies demonstrate that the person who jumps from one project to another takes approximately three times as long to finish as the person who single-mindedly executes

The Old Man plucked lightly on his quivering line. A slight nip. The rod began to bend then straightened as the fish released.

"It's a title," he replied. "Generally conferred by a king or queen to someone who rendered them service—though it can also be inherited. The title, though, means nothing. It's the person behind it that makes all the difference."

"How so?" the Boy questioned.

"None of the Great Ones started out 'Great,' Boy," the Old Man explained. "They became so because they made certain choices and paid the price that over time led to great accomplishments. Nothing was given to them for free, except the right to exercise their will, as we all have. Their greatness came at a cost that they paid willingly and would pay again because of who they became in the process. They chose big dreams over trivial pursuits and seldom waste energy sweating small stuff. We have but so much time, Boy, and the Great Ones use it in search of greatness. It all lies in their behavior as human beings—never in the title."

The Boy leaned toward the Old Man. "Are you a Great One?" he inquired in a timid voice.

The Old Man shook his head. "I am a messenger and your friend," he said. "No more. I was given certain gifts by those that came before me and in turn I pass those on to you. The Great Ones leave legacies that those of us who wake up can add to, if we choose the way."

The Old Man paused. "This, in some measure, I have tried to do."

The Old Man popped to his feet as beneath the surface an unknown fish struck his bait. With his left hand above his right he gauged the creature's strength, bent his knees to flex his legs, tightened the drag on his line, and pulled hard, though without

one project at a time until completion. To reach targets and accomplish big goals, you can't afford to waste that much time.

One of the Old Man's greatest lessons to the Boy begins early on, when he counsels him to not sleep walk, to think big, and to stop wasting energy on the small fry. Throughout the story, to the culminating moment of their last day together, the Old Man repeats the message in myriad forms, though his final act with the great fish proves his philosophy far more than words.

Focus on the prize. Go for it, and keep going for it with single-minded determination until you get it. Shoot for the bull's eye—and keep shooting.

Reference Chapters: 9, 20, 21, 30, 34, and 35.

strain. The line fell slack. The Old Man exhaled loudly and settled back into his spot on the rocks next to the Boy, who was already lost in his book.

The Boy stroked the smooth leather and marveled at the thinness of the pages covered with tiny writing—almost a thousand in total. He wondered what mysteries they contained and where they would take him. He couldn't wait to start reading.

He pulled the book onto his chest and stared into the Old Man's kind eyes and strong face. His friend, his very best friend—the best friend any boy could ever have.

"Thank you," he pronounced with a slight tremor in his lips.

A second rebel tear strayed from his eye before he quickly brushed it aside.

IX. *Thou shall demand integrity.*

"I hope I shall always possess firmness and virtue enough to maintain what I consider the most enviable of all titles, the character of an 'Honest Man'."

—George Washington

Chapter Sixteen

The box took up half the sideboard, covered in an oversized, white plastic bag with the word *Harrods* printed on the front.

The Boy served dinner, first his father, then his mother, propped by pillows in her special chair. He sat down across from his little brother and began to eat.

"I heard you made it a whole week without a single fight in school," his father began.

"No, sir—I mean, yes, sir," the Boy stammered.

"That's good," his father chortled. "Maybe you're finally learning something."

The Boy kept quiet.

"Even though I missed your day, I did pick up something in London," his father stated. He reached around and placed the box on the dining room table. "Since you're a year older now, I figured you might be ready for a man's game." He pushed the package toward the Boy. "I didn't have time to wrap it, but here it is."

The Boy pulled the box out of the plastic bag, a shiny top with images of soldiers holding muskets emblazoned across the front.

"It's a war game—based on world conquest and domination," his father preached, "the kind of stuff your ancient mariner buddy talks to you about."

Explanation of Edict IX

Pay careful attention to the following definitions of *integrity*:

1. Soundness of and adherence to moral principle and character; uprightness; honesty.

2. The state of being whole, entire, or undiminished.

3. A sound, unimpaired, or perfect condition.

These represent virtues by which to live and work and for which to constantly strive. Stand tall. Walk straight. Do the right thing, every time. Honor yourself and others. Don't settle. Show up. Give it your all.

I remember the day when, at age 3, my son Linus walked with me into the grocery store to pick up a fairly long list of supplies. As we marched down the aisles filling a cart, I pulled an oatmeal cookie from the open bin and gave it to him to keep him content. He happily rode around with me, finished the cookie, and by the time we reached the check-out line, I had completely forgotten about it. We unloaded the groceries into the car when I remembered the cookie. I picked up Linus and back to the same check-out line we went, where we stood and waited until the clerk got to us.

"You have no clue what the Old Man shares with me," the Boy thought. "Yes, sir," he said.

"If you get these dishes tidied up and put away, maybe I'll show you how to play," his father tempted.

The Boy resisted the urge to leap from his chair. He stood up slowly, deliberately refilled his father's wine glass, picked up the plates, and stepped into the kitchen, where he made himself his usual promise:

"I'll crush you," he muttered under his breath.

"As you can see," his father lectured, "the board is made up of six continents—North America, South America, Europe, Africa, Asia, and Oceania—each a different color."

He pointed at each one as he spoke. "Each continent is further subdivided into a number of countries—the bigger the continent, the more countries it has. The goal is to conquer the world by occupying all of the countries, or at least enough until everyone surrenders. Does that make sense?" the father asked.

"100 percent" the Boy thought. "Yes, sir," he said.

"At the beginning of the game, we will each be given an equal number of countries," his father continued. "Since there are three of us playing and 42 countries, we will each get 14, spread around the world. The object is to attack neighboring countries to those which you occupy, wipe out their armies, and take over, country by country, until someone controls most of the world. Clear so far?" the father asked in a mocking tone.

"Crystal," the Boy thought. "Yes, sir," he said.

"You will receive a number of armies to begin with and an additional amount each time it is your turn. Since there are three of us, we each get 35. Pick a color and count them out."

The Boy chose red, his brother blue, his father black.

"My son ate a cookie from the bin," I explained. "And we forgot to pay for it."

At first, the clerk looked at me as if I were an alien with two heads. As she perceived the clear and genuine intent, a warm smile embraced her face.

"Thank you," she said, simply. "I'm a little shocked—that's all."

"You're welcome," I answered, "though I wish you didn't feel that way. Have a great day."

Then we left.

Sadly, there are those who even now would think us foolish for our action, for not letting it go, who would easily justify the oversight—after all, "it's just a cookie."

I have learned that in no way is it ever "just a cookie." Integrity is a way of life, with immense, inherent power, where the universe moves in support of you, friends and colleagues appear when needed—and even when they don't—and where you yourself can tap an inner strength that propels decisions in the right direction toward the best possible outcome.

Lack of integrity acts as the X factor for failure. You never know where something will go wrong; and sometimes, in the outer material world, nothing shows. That seed of doubt, however—that little voice inside each one of us that does "know"—spreads its tiny roots and takes hold. It makes the next "oversight" easier. The next ethics compromise seems less problematic,

"Ah, the Commies," his father chuckled. "Let's see how long they last. Maybe you'll get China as a country, Boy—wouldn't that be perfect."

A small pile of armies rested in front of each of the players.

"The way you get more armies depends on three things," his father went on: "the number of countries you occupy, whether or not you control any continents and sets of cards—which I'll explain in a minute. Shuffle the cards, Boy," his father ordered, "and pass them out. Each one stands for a country and, whichever ones you get, that's where your armies go." His father began to snicker. "Sort of," he added.

The boys distributed their armies around the board, unsure of why or how.

"Now pay attention, 'cause here's how we fight." The father picked up the five dice, three red, two white. "One country is the attacker and another, the defender. They have to be next to each other. No country can ever be left unoccupied by less than one army, which means that the attacker can only roll as many dice as armies he can afford to lose, up to a maximum of three. In other words, if I have three armies on a country, and I'm the attacker, I can roll two dice only, because I can only lose two in order to leave one behind. Are you following me?"

Both boys nodded.

"The defender can likewise only roll as many dice as armies he can afford to lose, up to a maximum of two, but the defender wins all ties. If I have one army on a country and I'm the defender, I can roll one die. If I have two or more, I can roll two dice, and so on. Still with me?"

The Boys nodded again.

and the pattern establishes itself. The slippery slope turns ever slicker; and the end result is a long downward slide.

The causality that governs both the conspicuous and inconspicuous universe has infinite ways of manifesting its effects. The done deal sours. Your key employee gets an offer they can't turn down and leaves. The freeway runs through the neighbor's land and not the property on which you speculated that is now worthless.

As the saying attests, if you lie around with dogs, eventually, you will get fleas.

So what do you do when faced with a situation that calls for you to compromise your integrity?

Walk away. Not just once; every time.

What do you do if offered a sweet deal, an opportunity for easy profit, yet where the legality eases a tad too uncomfortably into the gray? Walk away.

What do you do if you have to compromise your own personal ethics to make a deal happen or to get a contract approved? Walk away.

What do you do if you know of impropriety and are suddenly faced with having to go along with "the program" or lose a valuable client? Let them go.

It will *never* prove worth it.

Interestingly, in the interviews conducted for *Modest to Millions*, this issue never came up in the normal course of discussion. I had to raise it every time. Why? Because,

"Example: If Brazil attacks Venezuela, I can throw three dice because I have four or more armies. Here goes . . . "

Six, four, two.

"Venezuela has three armies, so you could throw two dice, Boy—go ahead."

The Boy picked up the white dice and threw them. Four, four.

"You always take the top two dice and compare them," the father clarified. "In this case, my six beats your four, and my four ties your four, which means you would win that part, since defenders win the ties. You lose one army and I lose one. We keep playing until the attacker decides to stop—just like in real life. You've studied global history, right Boy?"

"Yes, sir," the Boy answered.

"Excellent. If the attacker wipes out all the defender's armies in a particular country, the attacker moves in." The father chuckled again. "Isn't that how it normally works in the real world?"

"Yes, sir," the Boy replied.

"That's pretty much it—a simple game, though one with a lot of strategy," the father admonished. "You have to think three or four moves ahead, something not so easy for you boys."

"Yeah, right," the Boy thought. "If I can beat you at chess, I can beat you here."

The father continued his annoying chuckle. "Let's play. Roll one die only and the highest roll goes first."

The father rolled a six and took the first turn.

"Alaska against the Northwest Territories, Boy. I'm kicking the commies out of the good ol' US of A. Rolling three versus two—show me what you got."

for those at the pinnacle of success, it was a nonissue; integrity was a given, not a subject that needed clarification. When finally asked, the ferocity of the answers on this point bears testimony to the inviolable nature of this issue. Act without integrity and out the door you send yourself, never again to be admitted to the inner sanctum—a personal, self-inflicted disgrace.

If you can't win with integrity, you simply can't win.

Life calls for many tough choices. At times, the best decision may be much tougher to make and the consequences in the short term may not appear to work in your favor. But the road to becoming a Great One is long; the allies you acquire along the way will grow in strength; the inner character you build for yourself will become unshakeable; and the result will ultimately manifest.

The Boy's first line-in-the-sand lesson from the Old Man shook him to the core and yet carried him all the way to the end. "I will have no friend who is a liar," the Old Man declared.

Ask yourself: What is your handshake worth? What do you want it to be worth? What are you going to do to make it worth that much?

Demand integrity, first of yourself, then of those around you. And if you play golf—don't move the golf ball.

Reference Chapters: 4, 8, 21, 27, and 32.

Roll after roll, the Boy watched his armies disappear. In less than an hour, the father wiped him out, laughing and drinking with each new conquest.

"You boys ready to surrender, yet?" he asked with a loud guffaw. "I guess your world history didn't help much today."

The Boy threw his cards on the board.

"Don't worry Boy—maybe you'll get lucky next time." His father grinned like a Cheshire cat. "Or maybe not. It does take a bit of skill, you know." He swallowed the last of his wine. "I'll tell you one secret. You've got to focus your efforts on taking one continent at a time—or you never have enough armies to continue. There's no way to scatter yourself around the globe and survive." He paused. "And isn't that just like life, too?" He paused again, gloating. "By golly, I feel like a philosopher."

The Boy picked up the pieces and returned them to the plastic containers that came with the box.

"Stay out of trouble, and you can take another shot over the weekend," the father provoked, "if you're man enough . . . "

"Count on it," the Boy thought, disgusted with himself. "Yes, sir," he said.

The Boy climbed dejected into his bed, the process of familiar self-flogging in full force.

"He creamed us," he told himself. "Not even close. What a loser," he disparaged, focused only on his personal failure. More than anything, he remembered the laughter, the mocking, the jokes that were not funny, mostly at his expense. They stuck to him like the smell of the shells of leftover mussels.

X. *Thou shall let go of past failures.*

"Virtually nothing comes out right the first time. Failures, repeated failures, are finger posts on the road to achievement. The only time you don't want to fail is the last time you try something. . . . One fails forward toward success."

—Charles F. Kettering

"This can't happen again," he exhorted. "I can never be that lame." On and on the vat of self-deprecation overflowed until he ran out of steam.

"Stop it," he demanded, both angry and deflated. "It was like this with chess at the beginning. You learned that and you can learn this, too."

He vowed to study the board after school.

By the weekend, he would be ready.

Explanation of Edict X

There are many definitions of *failure*—both formal and those that come from each of our own experiences. The dictionary includes the following:

1. The act or instance of failing or proving unsuccessful.

2. Nonperformance of something due, required, or expected.

3. An insufficiency; a subnormal quantity.

4. Deterioration or decay.

5. Becoming insolvent or bankrupt.

The definition of the verb *to fail* starts out with: "to fall short of success or achievement in something expected, attempted, desired, or approved . . ."

Take another moment to glance over the above, in such sharp contrast to the last edict's definitions of *integrity*. What benefit can possibly be derived by holding onto nonperformance, insufficiencies, deterioration, or falling short of success? And yet so many people do, mired in anger, bitterness, regret, and other negative mental conditions that occupy rent-free space in our minds and shut down our ability to aggressively move toward our goals.

Chapter Seventeen

The Boy placed his *bocadillo*, water, and towel in the small compartment below the mast next to the life preservers. He forgot his sunglasses though didn't care, content in his tan, floppy, Huckleberry Finn hat, white T-shirt, and matching shorts with the three blue stripes down the sides.

Pedro, the instructor, helped him rig his boat. They dragged it to the shore and into the water where Pedro gave the stern a sharp shove. "*Tu, sí puedes,*" Pedro encouraged. "You can do it."

The Boy gripped the railing, swept his leg over top of it and climbed into the boat. He secured the miniature jenny, pushed the centerboard beneath the surface, and grabbed the main line in his left hand, the tiller in his right. The canvas took and he moved forward with increasing speed.

He decided to sail out, even though most people walked because it was safer.

"I have to make it past the break," he willed.

Fifty feet away he could see the sandbar, where mountains of foam and surf came crashing down in a thunderous roar that drowned out all else. He said a brief prayer to the sea goddess, his face set in grim determination, his knuckles white on both line and rudder.

In *Jujutsu*, our *sensei* trains us to greet each opponent with the attitude that we are going to take them out—including the *sensei* himself, even though he is the highest-ranking black belt in the world today and hasn't lost a fight in at least 15 years. From day one on the mat, he relentlessly drills into each student the absolute need to forget about the last match and focus on the now, the immediate moment—what throw will you use, what grab, what technique, with no space whatsoever to wallow in a recent tough fall or the rough match of the last class.

To dwell on a past failure focuses our minds on one happening, one event, one negative point in time—one, and only one. The infinite possibilities of the future, the many potential solutions to a challenge, the thousands of options and different ways to achieve a goal—all of these instantly vanish. We play small—the exact opposite of "Great." Our dominant thoughts bring us back repeatedly to a dark state, a place of low energy that perpetuates itself. Past failures burden us, weigh us down, and eradicate all movement and flow. We can't see beyond the failure that acts like a giant filter that blinds us to the endless other possible outcomes. No greatness will ever come from such a negative place.

In conjunction with past failures, outside influences—even family members, friends, colleagues, peers, people that know about our foibles and remind us of them—can sap our strength and energy. If we

He remembered Pedro's words: "Turn into the wave and ride it out," he taught the Boy.

Forty, thirty-five, thirty feet.

"Maybe I'll catch it between swells," he hoped.

No such luck. A wall of water rose before him to block out the sun. Higher and higher it grew without pause and the Boy swallowed hard before pushing the tiller away and turning the bow to meet the wave. It burst over the boat like a giant waterfall and sent surging torrents over the Boy, down the sides of the boat, and out the back.

Just like that, it was gone.

The wind gripped the sail and the Boy was through, rapidly rising over the next swell and away from the churning surf.

"I did it," he yelled at the top of his lungs pumping his fist in the air. He glanced back at Pedro, who waved with a smile, turned, and walked away.

Awash in relief, joy, and excitement, the Boy let the tears that sprung from his eyes roll down his cheeks and onto his lips where they tasted of salt, like the sea water he now shook from his hair.

"I made it," he whispered out loud and, in that moment, for the first time, he savored freedom—the freedom the Old Man talked about, the freedom to go, to chart his own course, to fly. It felt alien and unusual, like a stiff formal shirt at a wedding. He only knew that he liked it and wanted more.

The Boy watched the color turn from light green to emerald to navy blue, violet, and almost black as the depths increased and the shore faded into the distance. He imagined the pirate ships that rested on the ocean's floor full of the treasures that sometimes washed up after a great storm. He marveled at the current rushing by, the tilt of the boat as it sliced through dark swells, and the

make the choice to let those failures go and move on, the naysayers and dream stealers will tire of repeating themselves to no avail. In fact, since no one wants to be made wrong, they may even come around and support us instead of appearing foolish for bad-mouthing someone who cannot be swayed. Comments made directly to us, such as, "You're not cut out for that" switch to commentary to third parties like, "there goes so-and-so, doing that thing again" and, finally, to "there's no point in even talking to them, they're just going to do what they do." Great!

It takes immense energy to build a successful enterprise; and the bigger the venture, the greater the output required. We can't allow ourselves the luxury of dwelling in self-made mental holding cells of worry and doubt. Remember that what other people think about you is none of your business. Stay focused and let the ne'er-do-wells go find some other victim to pick on.

Harping on past failures flies directly in the face of everything the Code represents. It means never taking responsibility in favor of casting blame. It denotes no patience, nor temperance. Courage and passion for success cannot live in the past, nor can discipline or single-mindedness.

On the positive side, failure represents the opportunity to begin again more intelligently. Failure teaches us

gentle hum from the hull when sail, sailor, and boat came together in that perfect harmony called "the groove."

For a time he sat and soaked it in, a strange, magnificent tranquility that gave rise to an odd feeling deep within him—simmering like a winter's broth on slow boil, begging to make itself known—a hint of confidence or a glimmer of hope.

He put his fingers in the sea, cool and refreshing, magical the way the rivulets of water flowed over the back of his palm like a stream over the tip of a boulder.

The Boy grew thirsty and in that thirst discovered hunger. He eased forward on the fiberglass bench, opened the storage hatch, and pulled out his sandwich and his water.

"*Chorizo*, butter, and *Manchego*," he divined with a grin from ear to ear. With driving zest he sank his teeth through the bread and the sausage and the thick slab of cheese to fill his mouth past its limits with the sandwich left hanging like a fish in a heron's beak.

"Wow," he mused. "If there is a heaven, it must be a lot like this."

He decided to sail toward the rocks to view them from the water, a perspective he had never enjoyed.

By and by he drew closer. The rocks jutted straight out from the sea as if to rudely interrupt the smooth lines of the coast on either side. They stood jagged and craggy, proud, defiant, and noble—a gray, wizened wizard with a long beard that reached into the swells at his feet.

The Boy spotted their special place, so tiny from a distance, yet mighty in its own way. He asked himself why the Old Man only fished on Sundays when he could go anytime.

what not to do going forward. It gives us experience that forms the basis for wisdom and a new outlook. We can draw from that knowledge with ever-greater confidence of impending success. Each failure—especially in business—creates a new barometer and compass to better guide us toward our targets. It acts as the fertilizer of our success.

Here's the challenge: Our improved compass only works if we absorb the experience, incorporate the learning, forget the failure, and engage again. There can be no "past" in a new beginning. Armed with our experience, we must start over—a new decision, a new commitment, a new plan, and renewed action. To do so, we *must* let go of past failures.

When the boat leaks, you get out and swim. If your horse dies, you dismount and walk. As the garbage truck drives away, you don't have to wave goodbye. Let it go, forget about it, move on.

The Old Man constantly reminds the Boy of how much energy he wastes by deliberating on the past, instead of creating his own future. He admonishes him to take what he has learned from his negative experiences and start anew—forget the failures and craft a new destiny.

The Great Ones become wise not because of their experience but because of their *capacity* for experience— the repeated process of embracing both success and failure,

"Doesn't matter," the Boy reasoned. "He never catches anything, anyway."

He realized that maybe he liked this boat even more than the rocks, or at least just as much, and felt a curious unease as if maybe, somehow, he were some kind of a traitor.

"Perhaps the Old Man could come with me one day," he flashed suddenly. "That would be perfect."

The Boy eased the bow upwind and set a course out to sea. He leaned back on his red bench and wrapped the main line around his big toe. He stared at the flutter of the sails backed by high, puffy clouds that flirted with a pesky blue sky and pulled his foot back and forth to avoid the luff, though in truth the flapping bothered him none at all.

As he made the final turn toward the *Club*, the evening swells calmed to a soft lapping. With the sunset on his shoulders, he navigated the quiet break, pulled the centerboard out of the sea, and glided all the way to the beach, where Pedro stooped to pull the boat onto the sand.

"You're a natural," Pedro praised. "*Muy bien hecho.*"

"I had a good teacher," the Boy beamed. "*Gracias.*"

As he wandered up the dirt road that led home, the glow stayed with him like a newfound friend or a shadow that only vanishes with the absence of all light. The clock tower chimed a quarter 'til. The Boy thrust his arms up in victory and broke into a jog, confident that he would make it before the top of the hour and avoid his father's wrath.

He felt his empty lunch pack slap rhythmically against his neck as he ran and relished the smile he would soon have to file away.

One thing he knew with certainty. Of his journey at sea, he would share nothing.

absorbing the learning, and moving forward toward greater achievements. The same winds that blow upon us all will always favor the most able navigators.

Reference Chapters: 1, 12, 16, 26, and 35.

Chapter Eighteen

"He destroyed me again," the Boy declared as he plopped onto his spot. "Wiped me right off the face of the map—though it took him two hours this time."

The Old Man passed him a *menta*.

"Do you know anyone on the local soccer team?" the Old Man asked.

"Yes, of course," the Boy replied. "Everybody does."

"And when do they play?" the Old Man continued.

"They play Saturday afternoons, all through the season," the Boy answered.

"And when do they practice?"

"On Wednesdays, usually, unless it rains." The Boy wondered where the Old Man was headed.

"Do you think the players of the great Barcelona practice more than once a week?"

"I'm sure," the Boy stated. "I'm sure they practice almost every day."

"Why?" the Old Man pushed.

"That's their job," the Boy retorted. "They get paid to practice."

"That's not the point," the Old Man admonished. "The point is that, to play at the higher levels, you have to work much harder. How do you think they became so good? Do you think they fell out of the crib with cleats on?"

XI. *Thou shall pay the price.*

"Grudge no expense—

yield to no opposition—

forget fatigue—till,

by the strength of prayer and sacrifice,

the spirit of love shall have overcome."

—Maria Weston Chapman

"No," the Boy mumbled, half-annoyed. "They probably played ball like everybody else until someone saw their talent, then put them on a team."

"Wrong," the Old Man corrected. "They didn't play like everybody else. When everybody else went home to watch TV, they stayed out and knocked the ball against the wall for a few more hours. When others went to birthday parties, they went to practice. They did things on a daily basis that others wouldn't do so that they could reach levels that most only dream about."

The Boy bit a hangnail off the tip of his index finger. A drop of blood oozed out. He flicked it away with his thumb.

"What's your point, Old Man?" the Boy complained. "I know you're going somewhere with this."

The Old Man sighed. "I find it odd that, after a few weeks with this new obsession, you somehow believe you should have already mastered it. That's kind of funny to me." He paused. "To beat your father at his own game, you're going to have to work much, much harder than ever before and decide whether you're willing to pay the price. Every master started out as a rank beginner, even the Great Ones."

The Boy wore a morose pout. He pursed his lips in silence and wrinkled the skin across his forehead.

"You don't have to make it so hard on yourself," the Old Man persisted. "Only arrogance keeps people stuck in trial and error. They fall down enough times to feel battered and quit without once seeking someone who has already walked the path they wish to travel. So foolish. So much more effective to get in the learning line early, ask questions, find out what helps and what hinders, uncover the pitfalls, study the shortcuts. Trial and error without guidance leads to much pain. Very few have the staying power to reach the top alone."

Explanation of Edict XI

I often get into heated debate with zealous advocates of the concepts that books like *The Secret* and *The Law of Attraction* put forth; not because I disagree with the basic theory, but rather because I have a much different opinion of what the authors intended to communicate than some of the commonly espoused doctrine. The notion that holding a thought causes it to magically manifest is absurd to me. No matter how long my wife thinks about a pearl necklace, for example, it is not going to ooze out of her pores and suddenly appear on her neck.

On the other hand, if a person *consciously chooses* to fixate on a pearl necklace as a dominant desire, opportunities will likely present themselves through which—assuming they take action—may ultimately result in the manifestation of that necklace.

The key words here are *opportunities* and *action*. We must remain open to the possibilities and, when a door opens, take the action, whatever that action is. Then, and only then, will we see results. *Paying the price* means taking action; the two go hand in hand. In fact, *paying the price means taking extra action*. There are all kinds of possible prices that we may need to pay for success—missing our child's sporting activity, arriving late to a family event, accepting an unfavorable handicap on the golf course, passing on the boys' or girls' weekend, foregoing the theatre or a night out of bowling, and

The Boy scratched his chin. "What does that have to do with me, Old Man?" he inquired.

"Have you read the rule book?" the Old Man nudged.

"What book? The instruction manual?" the Boy whined.

The Old Man nodded with a confident smile. "How can you expect to play the game well if you don't know the rules? Those books often contain tips and suggestions and will certainly open you up to other ideas. You might want to check it out."

"I finished the first chapter of the *Count of Montecristo*," the Boy shot back, defensive.

The Old Man nodded again. "Ahh, that's good," he said. "Just remember that, before the Count could win a battle on the field with his sword, he had to first win it off the field in his mind."

The Old Man's rod tipped down. He leaned forward for a brief moment until the rod rolled back up.

A shadow clouded the Boy's face, though not from the lack of sun. It came from that dark space deep inside—a place of rage and resolve where the desire for revenge masked the deeper hurt, kept the pain at bay, buried and untouchable.

"I'll pay," he muttered. "Whatever it costs."

Later that evening, the Boy tidied the kitchen quickly and retired to his room.

"Bedtime," his father soon shouted up the stairs. "It's a school night."

The Boy leaned out of his bunk and hit the switch on the wall that turned off the overhead lamp. After making the "hush" sign to his little brother in the lower bunk, he carefully eased the covers over his head, made a tent with his knees, and pulled the rules and his flashlight from their hidden spot under his pillow.

In his private cave he turned to page one.

so on. Paying the price means embracing the mental attitude to do whatever it takes at whatever the cost—and the highest levels of success will unquestionably extract a correspondingly high price.

To earn the rank of black belt in the practice of *Akayama Ryu Jujutsu*, it is made abundantly clear early on that a significant price will be demanded. You will first teach yourself how to fall, which means that, by definition, you will learn how to get up after you do. You will then be thrown to the ground with equal vigor—again requiring you to build your get-off-the-ground-and-fight muscle. You will likely enjoy blood on your uniform, bruised ribs and limbs, an injury or two, and ongoing aches and pains. After doing this for years, our *sensei* offers the following promise:

> "Though I truly hope that you never get into a real fight throughout your life, at least this once, you will know that you have."

That would be the day of the black belt test—an exercise in absolute survival during which fellow practitioners trounce you into oblivion, and your only hope is to pay the price, suck it up, and come out alive and relatively intact. Ironically, if you make it, you immediately pass from senior student at the top of the heap to the newest *sensei* at the absolute bottom of the pecking order.

Why would anyone go through that?

Chapter Nineteen

Day after day, the Boy went straight to the *Club* after school—
and as often as he could on the weekends. Only chores, homework, and Sunday afternoons with the Old Man precluded him
from his boat. He rigged it himself, stem to stern, and barely
needed help to drag the hull to the water's edge. Out to sea he
sailed, unconcerned with the break, heavy winds, or a dead calm.

He discovered that his fear of the big wave was just that—a
fear and no more, based on a creation in his mind and not the
danger in the surf, much like the black scorpion in the insect house
that the zookeeper showed him how to pick up by the tail and
render helpless. The boat always crested the wave if pointed
properly, even if it came down with a large crash on the back
side—a ride that gave the Boy a sense of power and conquest over
the elements.

He tacked and jibed, held tight courses upwind, and ran
downwind with his mainsail fat and wide. He ventured far into the
sea until the shore became a pencil-thin line on the horizon. In
brisk gusts he heeled the boat over and allowed the rail to run
through the water as he hung far off the opposite side, held by his
calves and the bend in his knees.

Now and then he pushed too far and flipped the boat. It
mattered little. Calmly, he stepped onto the centerboard, grabbed

Many people mistake the black belt for the goal itself. Not so. The black belt is a mere symbol of achievement. It represents the iron-will forged inside through the years of relentless effort punctuated by both joy and suffering. You wear it with pride and earn the knowledge that, unlike the majority who drop out, you were willing to pay whatever price called for to attain it.

You take the fall.

You get up.

You fight again.

You keep fighting . . . for as long as it takes.

No one passes the test without paying the price.

Price means that which must be given, done, or undergone in order to obtain something. In business, we pay the price to make one extra follow-up call after others stop dialing. We pay the price to stay in our office long past quitting time (notice that it is called *quitting* time—nothing that you or I want to be a part of). We pay the price to close one more sale than our colleagues, who have sauntered off to "Unhappy Hour," where they complain about why things are the way they have made them to be.

They say that misery loves company; but success loves company, too. Paying the price means doing what others are unwilling to do in order to have the things that others will never have. The only difference between ordinary and extraordinary is the *extra*. If you want extra, do extra, think extra, and learn to be extra. Pay the price.

the rail in his palms, and threw his weight toward the sea. The hull hesitated no more than a second or two before gently righting itself, sending a shower of salty water onto the Boy as the sail emptied over his head. He laughed, climbed on board, fetched the small plastic bottle with the bottom cut out from inside the storage hatch, and bailed out the excess sea water without concern.

Through the swells, the Boy found harmony; a magical convergence of wind, water, waves, and quiet; a tiny red sailboat gliding across a massive ocean; a boy lost in his thoughts who sat in silence, able to feel, to be, and yes, sometimes, to smile.

He looked often for the fish he seldom saw and reflected on the Old Man with his long bamboo pole that never seemed to work. Why didn't they jump more? Did they really swim beneath his boat? Not a single one showed itself, not ever. He pondered this world under the surface, a world without roads or buildings or cities yet just as alive—or so they said. Sometimes, his mind stayed blank, observing without regard for details, staring at the nothingness a calm ocean offers, happy to escape or at least grateful for a place that did not add to the hurt.

The dread crept over the bow with each final tack home. As he surfed toward shore on the inbound waves, his face adopted its familiar mask. He rinsed his boat, the sail, and his soul of any residue of joy.

Game time again.

Not surprisingly, those who work late quickly find out that the rank and file are no longer online or available by phone. It is not that hard, however, to connect after hours with CEOs, senior executives, or top producers. Go figure. And then some wonder why they get paid so much more than the average. It's not complicated. They produce more and work harder than the rest, *paying the price* long after the masses have moved on to the couch and remote control.

Notice how the edicts of the Code run together and work in harmony. *Paying the price* fits perfectly with *executing a plan* and *exercising discipline*. In addition to the action that goes with all three of the above, *paying the price* adds a mental element that further serves to breed the necessary confidence to never quit. When we embrace and accept that we are willing to pay the price, we send a powerful message to ourselves, both consciously and subconsciously, that says:

"I will till the land until I get the crop."

"I will smile and dial until I make the sales."

"I will challenge and better myself until I become the leader required to guide this team."

"I will seek out and master the skills I need for success."

"I will take the fall and get up as many times as needed or demanded of me."

"I will reach the goal, no matter what it costs."

Chapter Twenty

"You can't make a deal like that," the Boy cried out. "That's not fair."

"Life's not fair," his father laughed, "and the sooner you get that lesson, the better," he added, still chuckling. "Besides, people forge pacts in periods of war and have done so since the beginning of man."

The Boy glanced at his little brother, who kept his eyes fixed on the table. Although angry, the Boy couldn't blame him for making a truce with his father. The repercussions for refusing would be far too severe.

"Free move," his father added and pushed all of his troops from the European border across the Ukraine and Siberia until they sat, in a massive show of force in Kamchatka, poised for an assault on the Americas.

"You can't do that," the Boy exclaimed. "I thought a free move was only from one country to its neighbor."

"That's what I did, Boy," his father countered, "from one neighbor to another, in rapid succession, all across Russia. But if you know the rules better than me, I'll give you 60 seconds to show me."

Flustered, the Boy flipped through the rule book without success.

As Thomas A. Buckner once said: "To bring oneself to a frame of mind and to the proper energy to accomplish things that require plain hard work continuously is the one big battle that everyone has. When this battle is won for *all* time, then everything is easy."

Successful people simply comprehend and live this: Pay the price; do the work; and the results will come.

At the end of the day, one thing is certain: The only place where success comes before work is in the dictionary.

With his hands cut to shreds and covered in blood, the Old Man gave the Boy this crucial lesson. To win a great battle, pay the price. To achieve a great victory, pay the price.

In addition to all else, to become a Great One, *each of us must pay the price.*

Reference Chapters: 9, 12, 20, 24, and 35.

"If you want to play a man's game, you need to play like a man," his father sneered. "Place your pieces and let's go." A sly grin slit his face in half.

The Boy dumped his armies in Alaska. Without needing to defend his other borders, his father could focus his entire effort on taking the Boy's continent. If he did, the game was over. With no way to replenish his troops, the Boy would be whittled down to nothing. He passed the dice on.

"Well, Boy, it's time to get this party started," his father taunted. "From Russia to America, communists against the free world." He bellowed at his own paltry joke. "Rolling three against your two."

Again and again the Boy tossed the dice. Bitterly, he watched his armies dwindle away until only a single unit remained.

"You only have one man left," his father mocked. "Pity. My three dice against your one."

Six, three, two. The Boy rolled a four.

"I guess those Eskimos aren't so tough after all," his father declared, gloating like a fat pig after a joyous roll through a pile of muddy slop. "I'll just move my boys in, take a card, and turn it over to you."

The Boy stared at the board. His few remaining pieces were no match for his father's force and, though he knew his brother didn't want to fight him, neither could he escape through his brother's protected continents without a war that would leave him with nothing. If only he'd had more time . . .

"I surrender," the Boy ceded out of sheer frustration.

"And you always will," mocked his father as he raised his glass in toast. "Bet you thought you had me there, didn't ya' Boy?" he jested as he leaned back. "Maybe some other time," he added.

Chapter Twenty   **143**

XII. *Thou shall at all times persevere.*

"There are but two roads that lead to an important goal and to the doing of great things: strength and perseverance. Strength is the lot of but a few privileged men; but austere perseverance, harsh and continuous, may be employed by the smallest of us and rarely fails of its purpose, for its silent power grows irresistibly greater with time."

—Johann von Goethe

"And, then again, maybe not," his father bellowed with mirth. He let the board sit untouched, blaring at the Boy in defeat. His wine-stained lips painted a look like a jackal over a freshly killed antelope.

The Boy stored the pieces and muttered a shallow goodnight.

Buried under his covers, the Boy sifted through the passages in the manual.

"It's not here," he screamed mentally. "There is no rule about truces—I knew it," the Boy groaned and in that moment the Old Man's words echoed through his mind.

"You'll have to work harder than you've ever worked," the Old Man had admonished.

Angry and frustrated, more at himself than his father, the Boy began to crush the pages in his hands. He stopped, checked himself and his ire, and reached deep within to find his lost resolve and tap the dark side that fueled it.

"So be it," he promised finally, backed by a renewed iron will. He flipped to page one and began to memorize.

Explanation of Edict XII

The consensus choice for "most crucial quality" needed for success from the hundreds of businesses and billions of annually transacted dollars represented by the *Modest to Millions* interviews was virtually unanimous: perseverance—or some variation thereof such as persistence, tenacity, refusal to quit, unwillingness to give up, and so on. Time after time, interview after interview, this one trait dominated above all others—to the point where I had to pause and deeply reflect on its meaning and impact.

In asking the general question "What does perseverance mean?" we tend to hear certain pat answers such as:

"Stick with it."

"Never give up."

"One more try."

"Keep on keeping on."

While these responses denote our common ability to repeat oft-quoted lines, they do little to reflect an understanding great enough to fully embrace and utilize the power of perseverance. Before conducting the interviews, I, much like anyone else, had a cursory view of perseverance. I associated it with a fighting spirit, playing hard, winners never quitting, and the

Chapter Twenty-One

"He cheated," the Boy blurted out. "That's the only reason he beat me."

The Old Man settled back in his spot, his left hand lightly caressing the bamboo pole.

"And this surprises you?" he asked.

"No, I mean—it's just that . . . " The Boy caught himself. "I know—liars lie and cheaters cheat. That's their job."

"Not their job, Boy," the Old Man corrected, " . . . what they do—because of what they have become through their own choices. We can all choose otherwise, if we are awake."

The Old Man hesitated while the Boy brooded.

"No one is all bad or all good," he continued. "And we all embody both qualities. What we disdain in others are usually the traits we recognize in ourselves, particularly the ugly ones. Even a thief cares for his family and a murderer loves his dog. Our choices define who we become, not our intentions."

"I still hate him," the Boy spat.

"Perhaps you should revisit that, Boy. Did you hate him when he bought you a pellet gun? Did you hate him when he taught you how to shoot?" The Old Man scratched his chin. "Do you not see that sometimes you model his very same behavior? We all view the world through the filters we adopt over 10, 20, 50

like—without making any concerted effort to delve deeper.

The origin and root of the word *persevere* comes from the Latin verb *Perseverare*, which stems from the word *Perseverus*—which means "very severe or strict." The word *per* stands for "through," or "by means of." Definitions for *severe* include "harsh, serious, grave, rigidly accurate, conforming strictly to a rule, extremely plain or simple, unornamented, intense, difficult, rigorous." None of these terms suggest an easy ride, so it comes as no surprise that this would be the top quality of the super-successful—an obviously rare breed.

However, what I did find reassuring was that these descriptions did not include words like *talented, gifted, brilliant, genius, intelligent, evolved*—or any other trait reserved to a precious few by birth right. They spoke more to a mental toughness that is accessible to anyone. When it comes to perseverance, the only answer to the question "how long should I try?" or "how long should I continue?" is "Until"—until the job is complete, until the objective is realized, until the goal is met. There is no set timeline other than "as long as it takes."

I remember my mentor saying in one of our brainstorm sessions: "I'll take staying power over brain power every day of the week. Give me someone who just won't quit."

Too many people give up far too early in the game—often without realizing how close they are to a breakthrough when they stop. In that single act, they lose all of

years or more. To stay awake we must recognize that we don't know what we don't know and strive constantly to remove the blinders. Otherwise . . . "

"We become sleepwalkers," the Boy inserted. "Yeah, I know," he added, slightly insolent.

"Most would agree that it's important to have a dream. Few remember, especially when the going toughens, to wake up and make it happen. Not only that, every effort expended chasing bush-league fry is forever lost from the pursuit of a meaningful catch." The Old Man's tone intensified. "In that distinction rests the gap between winners and losers."

"Some people are too moronic to have a dream," the Boy argued, " . . . or too nasty. Why else would they behave the way they do?" The Boy spoke without conviction, as if to defend a point he recognized held little merit.

"To assume or presume shuts us down and I have more faith in you than that," the Old Man cautioned. "We must adopt and embrace other viewpoints and in so doing expand our minds to the possibilities—even of those we don't understand." The Old Man gazed at his line strung high over the rocks, lost into the blackness of the sea. "Can you do that, Boy?" he urged.

"I don't know," the Boy replied, hesitant. He bounced the heels of his sandals off the rocks and clicked the toes together. For a time, the dialogue ceased.

The Old Man placed his right hand on the Boy's shoulder, as if to add weight to his words. "You will beat him," he stated. "Though even in that there is great danger because no one likes to lose. The Great Ones understand that the only way to win is with grace, dignity, and humility. Naïve fools mock and taunt the losing side, forgetting that there will be other meetings on the field of battle."

the accumulated momentum that has led them to that point. Time will always be on our side when we make the decision that it doesn't matter. We will plug regardless of the chronological passing of minutes and hours. Only success matters.

We have all heard the story of the salesman who simply decides "I will not stop knocking until I make a sale"—only to have that happen at 11:30 PM. Even though we likely hear about it because it makes a better spin than the sale at 4 in the afternoon, the principle still applies. Somehow, in an almost mystical way, the universe conspires to support the person with dogged determination who, like the Little-Engine-That-Could, keeps on chugging. *The beauty about perseverance is that it is simply a decision*; it does not require special skills or apply to a uniquely chosen group. If you want it, get after it and stay after it—plain and simple.

Virtually all of the edicts of the Code define and explain aspects of mental toughness, all of which, at the end of the day, fit either directly or tangentially within perseverance.

Beginning with Edict I—we must first make a committed decision. The process of "committing," however, is not a one-time, static event. We must recommit repeatedly and *persevere in our commitment* in order to stick with the decision.

Second, we conceive and execute a plan. As we analyze the results, we reconceive and *persevere in our*

The Old Man leaned closer. "'To the victors go the spoils,' the saying goes. Few people grasp that the 'spoils' include ego, arrogance, and the cause for future defeat. Of this we must be very wary." The Old Man rocked back.

"Are you ever going to catch a fish, Old Man?" the Boy interrupted, growing tired of the lecture. "It's not as if you don't get enough bites . . . "

The Old Man did not respond. He settled his posture, reached up with his left forefinger and tested the slack, turned, and spoke in a stern voice.

"I have only one more question, Boy," he imparted, without wasted breath on the Boy's outburst.

The Boy's head snapped around. He wondered if he had offended the Old Man.

"Are you doing the work?" the Old Man demanded.

The boy reached into his back pocket, pulled out the rules book, and waved it at the Old Man, defiant.

"Good," the Old Man assented.

execution. We relentlessly repeat the process until we attain the stated goal.

Third, we take full responsibility. This is a never-ending process, a daily undertaking in the face of myriad challenges and setbacks that requires us to *persevere with a spirit of personal accountability*. It never stops. The Great Ones blame no one.

Then we embrace patience and temperance, not sometimes—always. We must *persevere in stillness through our moments of ire and overzealousness*.

Acting with courage requires us to wage a perpetual battle with our fears—*persevering despite the deepest and darkest demons* that plague us from time to time. As the inner devils appear—and they will—we persevere to outlast them. As it does in a romantic partnership—passion will fade over time. Only *perpetual nursing and cultivating* will keep it alive, thriving, and regenerating.

The willpower needed to exercise discipline can seldom take a break. A tiny slip or failure to do what must be done can have disastrous consequences. We must *persevere uninterruptedly with both disciplined thought and disciplined action* to drive the energy flow toward our targets. To remain single-minded, we must resist all distractions and *persevere with a laser-like focus*. Integrity cannot exist in isolation on Sundays or on a part-time basis. We must *persevere in our choices* to maintain ethics at all time—an absolute requirement for success at the highest levels.

Chapter Twenty-Two

The Boy rode up the front part of the vast swells, over the crest, and down the back, gliding above the hues of violet, inky blue, and shades of black that marked the bottomless Mediterranean in fluid convergence. Steadily, he memorized the rules, recited them out loud, and shouted them as if he were Plato or Socrates speaking to the endless ripples that spanned in all directions, his minions that hung on his words of victory. Far out to sea he ventured, to a place known only to him, where his face softened to allow other truths and the vast expanse offered its wisdom and dared him to dream.

The sea gifted him with serenity and showed him the insignificance of all beings—how, without a trace or a memory, it could swallow us all. Despite the boundless grandeur, he remembered the Old Man's caution—that without us there is no world, the paradox of the cycle of life.

He thought about his friend the Old Man, the sleep walkers, the Great Ones, and all else between and wondered where he might fit.

"Could he do it?" he asked himself. Could he become something, take the great castles he built in the sky, and sink a piece of them into the rocks?

"Could he do it?"

To let go of our failures, we must constantly refuse entry to negative chatter, block out the busts, isolate the moments of loss, and *persevere in ever-lasting positive self-talk* that does not allow pity, wallowing, or floundering in the past.

And, finally, we pay the price. And then we pay it again. And we keep on paying, *persevering in our choice to pay*, until we win.

The immortal, almighty perseverance encompasses all.

On a small how-to note, at my seminars, I am often asked the following question: "It's all fine and good that business giants have this innate quality—what can I do to develop a persevering nature?"

Here's the answer: "Start small, finish the job."

Build your perseverance muscle in increments by completing the tasks you set for yourself all the way to the end. If you set a goal to make 10 prospecting calls, don't stop after call number 9. If you decide to comb your file cabinet for potential leads, start at the front of the top drawer and cull the entire unit—until the back of the bottom drawer. If you develop a hankering to clean your office, then brew a strong pot of coffee on a Saturday morning and tidy and organize until your desk sparkles.

Finish the job. In so doing, you will get used to completing things, sticking with tasks, and not stopping prematurely. Over time, this becomes a habit, a way of acting that will naturally build the nature of perseverance

The question dangled like the sinking sun that appeared each morning with a promise of possibility, then taunted and provoked before vanishing at the end of the day.

"Could he do it?"

He toyed with the maybe, grasping to a shred of hope, unwilling to let it anchor for fear that it might turn into the albatross around his neck that forever plagued him with a reminder of what could have been.

He sailed and sailed, jousted with warrior gods, danced with fair princesses, and partook from the rich table of his imagination a feast that knows no limits in its abundance.

Yet when the ship turned to shore, a certain famine set in, the once soft, summer-like features slipped on their cold winter coat, his eyes that briefly sparkled like emeralds turned to gray slate and the dreams, like the light foam from the evening waves, evaporated.

Chapter Twenty-Two   **155**

that we all have within us. We've had it since we were babies and wanted to crawl; then learned to walk; then rode a bike. Most of us have forgotten that we truly can *decide to be successful.* From that point on, it's all about *perseverance.*

Month after month, unbeknownst to the Boy, the Old Man lets go of all small fish in favor of one final, great battle. In so doing, he sets the Boy up for his most important and transformational lesson: the immense power of perseverance to achieve any monumental feat, including the fulfillment of a life-long quest to become a Great One.

I leave you, respectfully, with my favorite quote from Napoleon Hill—one that has made the greatest impact on this work and that, for me, says it all:

> *"The majority of people are ready to throw their aims and purposes overboard, and give up at the first sign of opposition or misfortune. A few carry on despite all opposition, until they attain their goal. These few are the Fords, Carnegies, Rockefellers, and Edisons. There may be no heroic connotation to the word 'persistence,' but the quality is to the character of man what carbon is to steel."*

> —Napoleon Hill

Chapter Twenty-Three

The early stages unfolded in the usual way, each player vying to occupy continents and secure the flow of extra troops—the life-blood of the game. The Boy ended up with the two small ones, South America and Australia, while his little brother took Africa and his father North America—a relatively balanced division that gave them all about the same number of armies at the beginning of each turn. They divided Europe and Asia between them—two continents with far more borders and much more difficult to hold.

The cat and mouse repartee began, with all players building the reserves on their border nations to protect their continents and watching for someone to make a major move. For each army that his father placed in Central America, the Boy added one in Venezuela to create a stalemate.

The Boy felt certain that his father would attempt to cheat, as he did last time, to lull him into a false sense of security or trick him with a fancy, cross-continent free move. His father didn't know that he, the Boy, had mastered the rules. If he could anticipate and figure out his father's ruse, with a classic bait and switch, he could set him up.

They played a few rounds, swapped countries in Asia, no one engaging in any major risks. The Boy noticed his father starting to build forces in Greenland, poised, it appeared, for an attack on Iceland, a country occupied by his brother as part of the European continent.

In the birthing of a Great One, "persistence" or "perseverance" is that carbon. May the forging begin. . . .

Reference Chapters: 18, 29, 31, 34, and 35.

"Wait," the Boy divined, "what if he is amassing troops without any intention of attacking Europe, thinking that I won't notice, and intending to free move them all down to Central America to attack me? His plot would catch me without time to increase the defenses needed to protect my continent. If he tries to do that, though, his armies will be isolated. What if . . . " the Boy's mind whirred, " . . . what if I pretend to ignore the threat, add a few troops of my own, and wait?"

The Boy's brain swam with excitement. He casually added two armies to Venezuela and brought his total there to eight, versus the six his father had in Central America. He then reinforced Brazil, put the rest of his armies in Siam, and took China before passing the dice. Through Japan, which he already occupied, the Boy held adjacent territories all the way from Australia to the Russian border of Kamchatka—a striking point into North America.

His father placed more armies in Greenland, ignored Central America, and, after kicking the Boy out of meaningless Mongolia in central Asia, attempted his ploy:

"Three turn truce between Greenland and Iceland?" the father asked his little brother, who nodded. "Well, in that case," he said as he reached for his armies, " . . . I'll move all these men South for a happy rumble in the jungle." He chuckled as he started to push his troops down the Eastern seaboard of the United States. "I can't believe you fell for it again, Boy."

The Boy's face turned into a contemptuous smirk. He could scarcely contain his enthusiasm. Though his father had 14 armies in Central America to his 8 in Venezuela, the Alaskan border was left unprotected. His turn was next and he could sacrifice all his reinforcements to get into Alaska, knowing that he could back them up later through a free move up the Eastern Asian seaboard—

A Brief Amendment: Inferiority and Deserving

"Nothing in the world can take place of persistence.
Talent will not;
nothing is more common
than unsuccessful individuals with talent.
Genius will not;
unrewarded genius is almost a proverb.
Education will not;
the world is full of educated derelicts.
Persistence and determination alone are
omnipotent."

—Calvin Coolidge

and use his father's own technique to wipe him out, before his father even had a chance to attack. Deliberately, he counted his countries.

"Seventeen countries—divided by three is five armies." The Boy paused for effect. "Plus two more for Australia and an extra two for South America—hmmm, I wonder what I can do with them all." He feigned to scan across the board.

"Let's see," the Boy continued. "Let's put this first one in Kamchatka . . . and maybe this second one . . . and maybe—oh heck, let's put them all there." He dumped all his troops in the same spot—his 14 armies against his father's 6.

"Alaska's looking mighty thin, yessiree," he added in an annoying sing-song voice, " . . . might have to pay the igloos a visit." The Boy gloated and rubbed it in thick.

Briefly, the Old Man's voice whispered softly: "The Great Ones win with grace . . . " it said.

The Boy disregarded it in a blink. He had waited too long for this moment and would milk it for all it was worth.

"Kamchatka against its northern neighbor," the Boy directed, " . . . and I'm rolling three."

Though each side lost a few troops, the six armies in Alaska were no match for the Boy's superior numbers. He wiped them out and moved his men in, every one except the mandatory single army that had to stay behind.

"For my free move, I'll send over a few Brazilians for extra support." The Boy took seven armies from Brazil and placed them in Venezuela as reinforcements, an extra army over his father's numbers—except that now his father had lost his continent and would need all his troops to reclaim it.

On the next turn, his father received only four armies. He rolled against the Boy until he depleted his forces and had to stop.

As I mentioned in the introduction, the Code came together from the teachings gleaned from the interviews of hundreds of highly successful individuals. They embody the character traits and action steps constantly referenced as the causes for significant financial success.

In addition, two other insights stood out that applied to the ultra-successful—those with tremendous net worth, who made their first fortune in a core business and thereafter expanded to embrace many other ventures in diverse industries, often with even greater success. These financial titans represent the modern day Carnegies, Rockefellers, Rothschilds, Morgans, and so on.

First, *they are NEVER satisfied*. They never rest on their laurels, never kick back and let their shops haphazardly flow, and never stop seeking how they can improve, get better, compete harder, extract more. Often, the hunger that fuels this motivation *comes from an inferiority complex or a dark side*— one which they readily acknowledge is a positive driver for success. I heard stories of monthly nightmares, cold sweats, chips on the shoulder that never disappear, deep-seeded ire, and more—all of which adds timber to a fire that, on a daily basis, continues to roar. Those of us who suffer from periodic doubt or other lack of self-esteem should welcome the fact that, if well-channeled, that very doubt can propel us to our highest aspirations.

On his turn, the Boy received ten replenishments and put them all in Venezuela. His father's force looked suddenly less impressive and the Boy gave no quarter. He obliterated his father in three rolls and controlled North America on two fronts. His father would never get it back and, therefore, would lose the extra armies with which to fight the Boy, who began to hum and bob his head in a mocking taunt.

His father wrinkled his brow, bent over the game board, looked up at the Boy, back at the board, and glanced away as if he had a sudden realization.

"You set me up, Boy," he barked in a vicious, ugly tone. "You knew all along that I would make the free move, that you would dump your men in Russia, and that my men would be stuck. You were waiting for me to bite so you could take me out."

The Boy ignored the warning signs, raised his eyebrows, and smirked. "Just playing by the rules," he jested. "It's your game."

His father's face morphed into a nasty, Iguana-like creature, red with rage. "This game is over," he yelled as he picked up the board and dumped the pieces onto the dining room table. "Pick it up and put it away," he howled as he slammed the board down, shoved his chair back, and stormed out of the room.

The Boy could not repress his twisted joy. He scowled ear to ear at his little brother. "Told you," he mumbled under his breath. His brother timidly smiled back.

The Old Man's words lay dormant in his subconscious. Delirious with glee, he wallowed in the feeling of conquest, did a victory dance in his head, and fell asleep as the spectators cheered for him, *El Gran Campeón,* the Grand Champion, and shouted his name.

For the first time in many an eve, the nightmares did not come.

Chapter Twenty-Three   **163**

No one applauds when a billionaire makes another million—not us, not them, and not their peers. It's just "what they do"; and their relentless quest for improvement should stand as a lesson to us all. In a world where the one guarantee is change, the only guard against it is for each of us to stay ahead of it—to fortify and add constantly to the fortifications, both within our operation and with each member that plays on our team. If we can use a bit of inner fear to keep us moving, then so be it.

Second, another astonishing discovery (at least to me) was the concept that, in order to accumulate wealth, each of us would first need to believe that we "deserve it." Otherwise, we would find ways to sabotage our potential success, keep a lid on our earning potential, crash into self-created ceilings within our mental comfort zone, and never make it into the big leagues, or rapidly fall out of them after a momentary appearance. More often than not, that feeling of "deserving" surfaced over a protracted period of time and years of toil.

The word *deserve* stems from the Latin root *deservire*, which means "to serve diligently." In other words, the more people we diligently serve, the greater our reward for so doing. Consider carefully that those who impact the most people have since forever been paid the most— actors who impact millions on the silver screen, athletes who live in the public eye, CEOs whose companies supply the masses, inventors that modernize our way of living, and so on. A direct correlation exists between

Chapter Twenty-Four

"Your report card came in," his father said in an insolent tone that the Boy instantly did not trust.

"Oh?" the Boy commented, uneasy.

"If I'm reading it correctly, it appears as though you got a C in mathematics," his father stated as he flipped the two-page booklet at the Boy.

The Boy glanced at his grades. "So?" the Boy responded, ". . . the rest are all As and Bs."

"So a C is not good enough, Boy," his father declared with a triumphant, sadistic sneer. "It seems to me that you've been spending too much time navigating to Mallorca and not enough time studying." His father paused for effect. "So, effective immediately, your little toy will simply stay on the beach until the next report card—and it best be an improvement if you ever plan on sailing again."

"Over one C," the Boy half-shouted, "you're taking my boat away?"

His father gloated as he shook his head. "And if you sass me, Boy, I'll forbid you from seeing old Fishless Joe."

"But . . . ," the Boy protested before his father wagged a finger in the air and cut him off.

"One more word, Boy . . . " his father threatened.

number of people served and the level of income of an enterprise. This begs the question of how do we build the belief that we "deserve" to be successful?

The answer lies in the relentless application of the Code. If you make and stick to your decisions, execute properly conceived plans, take full responsibility over an extended period of time—with courage, passion and integrity—*and* pay the price through single-minded and disciplined action with no time line other than however long it takes, then your wealth will naturally follow, with every penny well deserved. At the end of the day, it boils down to intelligent, unrelenting hard work.

Those who aspire to be Great Ones need look no further than the Code. With a persevering attitude and an absolute refusal to ever quit, in due course the results are a foregone conclusion. There are no free lunches—only fools who look for them.

May you be blessed with the work ethic necessary to create your fortune.

End of the Code
(*story continued . . .*)

Stunned into silence, the Boy stared at the partially eaten flank steak that floated on his plate in a pool of its own blood.

"He took my boat away over a single C," he repeated to himself, incredulous, and in that instant he knew better. He flashed on the livid red face two days before, the dumping of the game pieces all over the dining room table, and his own behavior throughout it all.

"He couldn't take losing," the Boy realized with a sinking heart, " . . . he's never cared about my grades."

Ashamed and defeated, the Boy chewed the meat with distaste, never looking at his father, his own saliva mixing with the blood that helped him tap the dark space. Slowly, like a volcano that scorches far beneath the ground before it erupts, deep within him the ugliness commenced to boil.

Chapter Twenty-Five

The Boy's rage sweltered throughout the week. He woke on Saturday and, like an automaton, emptied his piggy bank into his light blue Adidas bag, added a ball of twine, stuck his lighter in his trousers, and slipped out of the house after breakfast.

He made his way down the long hill and turned right by the railroad tracks. He followed the dirt road to the town's only factory, where they manufactured rockets for the firework displays that happened during the fiestas three times each year.

He knew the shop would close at noon on the weekend, arrived well before that, and purchased six large rockets with long sticks—of the kind packed with gunpowder that lit up the night with a colossal thunder clap at the end of each show—and a slow-burning fuse, all of which he deposited in his bag.

Like a robot, he hiked back up the hill and down the street to the orchard next to the football field. He squatted below an olive tree, removed his purchases from the bag, snapped the long sticks off at the base of the explosives, and turned them all so that the fuses faced inward. He wrapped the bundle of rocket heads in twine and bound the fuses around the top of the slow burner he had bought an hour earlier.

With an eerie casualness, he climbed down the retaining wall, found a crack near the base large enough for his contraption, bent over to wedge it in carefully, pulled the lighter from his pocket, and lit the fuse.

He retreated 30 yards to stoop behind an overgrown *algarroba* trunk and waited.

The bomb blew with a shocking fury, sending the stones that made up the wall soaring high into the sky and the dirt cascading into the water drainage ditch that filled quickly and spilled over onto the road.

The Boy watched as the dust settled, picked up his bag, scrambled up the bulbous mound he just created, and continued up the mountain behind the orchards to the Cross where he sat, with vacant eyes that gazed listless over the Mediterranean until the setting sun chased him home to the belt that he knew would be waiting.

Book 3

The Journey

"I girdled Asia, bore her blows,

Her summer suns, her winter snows,

Trod plain and hill from Rum to Ch'in;

Yet all I learnt I found within."

—Arnold J. Toynbee

Chapter Twenty-Six

"They're sending me away," the Boy stated.

"I know," the Old Man admitted as he cut the strips of aloe from the leaf in his bag. "To the monks, right?"

"Yes," the Boy answered, " . . . to the monastery at El Escorial, outside Madrid, with the *Agustinos*."

"They're tough," the Old Man declared.

The Boy shrugged his shoulders.

"When do you leave?" the Old Man asked.

"The day after tomorrow," the Boy answered.

The Old Man's ancient fingers stretched the aloe along the length of the cracked scabs. "So soon . . . " the Old Man mulled.

The Boy pulled his shirt down, took his spot, and clicked his sandals nervously against the rocks. The Old Man adjusted his seat, ran his hands up the bamboo pole between his knees, and began to tap. The Boy noticed immediately and kept quiet.

"Certain things I feel I must share with you, Boy," the Old Man broached, " . . . as it may be a while before we see each other again."

The Boy nodded.

"We have spoken many times of 'fresh starts,' like when you shot your brother, climbed the forbidden tree, or entered the village school." The Old Man stroked his reel and kept tapping. "There is an aspect of which I have not told you."

The Boy glanced sideways at the Old Man.

"Unfortunately—or perhaps it is simply the ways of nature—we only get so many fresh starts until by mysterious fate they somehow run out."

The Old Man paused. "Not because people can't get up from a later fall but rather because the law of accumulation applies to all of us in both a positive and a negative way. Too many bad choices dig holes almost impossible to climb out of and ingrain patterns too difficult to change. Take the loving mother who habitually runs behind and drives too fast to an important appointment. She watches the stoplight ahead turn yellow and seeks to beat the red, just as the *camión* coming from the opposite direction times the change to green. In a split second she is dead and her children grow up alone."

The Old Man sighed. "Or the young person that has a brush with the law and on the first violation receives probation, only to discover that the second or third offense leaves them to contemplate their antics from inside prison walls. And so on."

The Old Man turned toward the Boy. "At some point careless must become cautious and better choices must be substituted for poor ones. You are in a precarious position, Boy," the Old Man admonished.

The Boy frowned.

"In all likelihood, your father has spoken to the monks and told them that you are a 'challenged' or a 'problem child.'"

The Boy stared at his toes.

"They will scrutinize you and watch you carefully, predisposed to think the worse."

The Old Man pulled lightly on his pole. "Still, human beings are fickle and everyone wants to make up their own mind. If you stay humble and act kindly, they will likely draw their own conclusions and utter comments like: 'He's not so bad—he needed a new environment' and so on. On the other hand . . . " the Old Man cautioned, " . . . if you act foolishly and give them reason to validate their predisposition, they will treat you with much harshness and give you no quarter whatsoever. My point is this . . . "

The Old Man spoke in a somber tone. "I believe this may be your last fresh start . . . "

The Mediterranean breeze tickled the Boy's nostrils and the sea air coated his lips with salt.

"I'm a little scared," the Boy finally confessed.

"Sure," the Old Man agreed. "That is normal and understandable—though remember that you are never alone."

"What do you mean?" the Boy queried.

"Whenever I face a challenge, I talk to my mentor," the Old Man suggested.

"How can you do that?" the Boy countered. "You told me your mentor passed years ago."

The Old Man smiled. "His physical self moved on, yes. His wisdom, energy, and spirit live with me every day. Whenever I need help, I seek him out. I ask myself, what would he do under these circumstances—what would he say to me if he were here, what counsel would he offer? And so we talk and he aids me in making the right decisions whenever I need support".

The Old Man plucked his line out of custom. "When you stand before a threat, a challenge, or a quandary, ask yourself this one, key question, Boy: 'What would the Great Ones do?'"

The Boy did not answer, floundering in a pool of confusion and mixed emotions.

"Though these hands are old and twisted," the Old Man added, " . . . if you write to me, I will write you back . . . "

A brief light flickered over the Boy's face. "I will, Old Man," he stated with emphasis. "I surely will."

The sun and the Old Man's words sank together. As they stood to take their leave, the Old Man squared up in front of the Boy and placed his palms on the Boy's shoulders. For a moment, the Old Man's kind eyes looked profoundly into those of the Boy. Then he spoke with firm confidence:

"You can do it, Boy," he urged. "Make me proud."

The words hung heavy like a sodden winter coat as the Boy trudged up the long hill toward his house.

"A last fresh start . . . you can do it . . . make me proud," the Old Man said, and the Boy wondered if he could. His father wouldn't be there to beat him and put him down, he reasoned, and, if he couldn't do it for himself, perhaps he could do it for his friend—whatever "it" is.

"Maybe things can be different this time," the Boy sought to convince himself.

Maybe.

Chapter Twenty-Seven

The Boy's brow bounced rhythmically off the window as the train made its way across the Spanish plains and into Castilla. He had cried without pause from Tarragona to Valencia, where he made the switch to the inbound line without incident.

"I really hope you can turn yourself around," his father said at the station, though it sounded shallow and uncaring—nothing like the warm words of encouragement he received from the Old Man.

He boarded the platform without looking back, though his feigned indifference did not stop the tears that flowed freely and in abundance before they dried out somewhere past Almería and he felt nothing. His head danced in staccato against the glass, tapping on the pane like the Old Man's fingers on the bamboo pole. In a few short hours he would reach Madrid, where his dorm master would meet him to drive or switch to a local commuter to complete the final phase of the trip.

He dozed. In his dream he sailed far out to sea where a ferocious storm came upon his boat—waves taller than his mast, high winds, and pelting rains. With his senses on full alert, he manned the tiller, rode the waters to their fluid pinnacles, and swooshed down the back sides like a surfer, over and over, until the wrath played out. He arrived on shore tired yet elated, exhausted yet empowered from his victory, drenched, with his face all a grin, to a cheer from his friend Pedro who helped him put up the hull.

The train's horn woke him from his revelry. In a daze he read *Estación de Madrid* on the sign that flew by as the brakes began to squeal and the wheels slowed to a stop.

He spotted a priest with a closely cropped beard in a long brown smock obviously looking for someone. He waved and the man waved back as he walked toward the Boy.

"I'm Father Jose María," the man hailed with a smile. He held out his hand. "How was your trip?"

"Good," the Boy said as he shook it, " . . . though I'm a little tired."

"Of course," the priest replied. "Let me help you with your bags."

"So far, so good," the Boy noted mentally. "He seems friendly enough."

"I brought the van," the priest went on, " . . . to make it easier for us. We can ride out together and I'll show you a few things."

"*Gracias*," the Boy answered politely.

"Our town is at a higher elevation than the city," the priest explained. "It's usually about ten degrees cooler. The king liked to look down on a clear day and behold his palace in Madrid."

"Oh," the Boy responded, suddenly interested.

"Almost a kilometer above the monastery, the king's men carved a massive throne into the stone so that his majesty could oversee the construction," the priest continued. "You can hike up to it and check it out for yourself—even sit in the king's chair." The priest paused. "If you have privileges, that is . . . " he added.

"What's that?" the Boy exclaimed loudly as he spotted a cross far in the distance between two mountain peaks.

The priest laughed. "That's the Valley of the Fallen, a monument to the soldiers who defended the Christian faith. It's one of the largest crosses in the world—150 meters tall and 60 meters wide—and can be seen from as far as 75 kilometers away."

"Wow," the Boy thought. "That's more than three times the size of the cross at home." He turned to the priest. "Can you climb up to it?" he asked him.

The priest laughed again. "No, son, it's restricted by a fence. The base is made up of a square concrete building that houses a museum, an amphitheater, and a basilica that we'll visit later this fall on a field trip. You'll see."

The Boy gazed through the windshield as the van made its gradual ascent of the low-lying mountains. The hills seemed greener and more lush, with stands of pine and crops he didn't recognize.

Father Jose María interrupted his daydreaming. "I feel that it's my duty to tell you how things work around here," he shared without malice.

The Boy questioned what would come next.

"We have 40 boys in your class, half from the local village, 15 more from Madrid that go home most weekends, and a few, like yourself, who come from far away. I spoke with your father . . . "

The Boy's heart skipped a beat.

" . . . and wanted to let you know that everyone who visits San Agustín is treated with a clean slate."

The Boy breathed a sigh of relief.

"If you act properly and do your work," the priest continued, " . . . you earn privileges. If you don't and misbehave, you will be punished and placed on a leash that will be tightened as much as we deem necessary."

The Boy wondered whether the leash was literal or figurative. "That sounds very fair," the Boy remarked.

"Yes it is," the priest agreed. "We pride ourselves on fairness and justice and will go to great lengths to protect both." He paused for a moment, then spoke in a stern though nonaggressive tone. "What I'm saying to you is that, from now on, you control your fate completely. What you make of this journey with us is entirely up to you. We begin by believing the best of you."

The voice of the Old Man echoed to him in silence: "One last fresh start . . . "

"*Gracias,*" the Boy repeated, relieved though still anxious at what else might lie in store.

"Ah," the priest stated. "Here we are at the bottom of our hill. The king had it lined this way with trees on both sides so that he could enter in full regalia in his carriage followed by his noblemen. The monastery rests exactly one kilometer from here."

Up they went. The Boy flashed on the hill in Altafulla that led from the railroad tracks to the church tower, not so different from this one, except for the trees.

"On the left are our sports fields," the priest shared, "where you will spend most afternoons playing *fútbol* or tennis or basketball. We even have a swimming pool that opens in the spring." The priest glanced sideways at the Boy. "That is of course unless you are castigated . . . " The priest let the sentence hang.

"What happens then?" the Boy queried almost unconsciously.

"Then you will be detained in the monastery for the length of your punishment and forbidden to leave," the priest informed. "We find plenty for you to do . . . "

The massive structure loomed greater as they grew closer, larger than anything the Boy had ever seen—much larger.

The priest grinned at the look on Boy's face. "Impressive, isn't it?" he commented. "It's almost the size of four *fútbol* fields and the outer walls measure six meters thick. The esplanade spans one hundred meters wide and three times as long on two sides, with tunnels under most of it. The formal gardens are in the back."

Groups of tourists gathered and took photographs, vendors lined the sidewalks, and a horde of boys kicked a soccer ball in an obvious friendly game.

"Those are some of your classmates," the priest pointed out. "They are in recess. You will meet them for the first time at lunch."

The Boy nodded. He glanced at the gigantic complex, the austere façade, and the stone esplanade that he knew would be as dark and lonely at night as it was two hundred years ago.

"How long?" he asked himself, "how long would these giant walls be called 'home'?"

Chapter Twenty-Eight

The Boy followed Father Jose María into his dormitory—two long, rectangular rooms severed by stone archways and split down the middle by a partition, against which stood rows of neatly made beds separated by dark brown bedside tables.

"Since you just arrived," the priest began, " . . . this will be your bed." He pointed at the last one, a bare mattress over a set of box springs. "Your bedding will be brought later," he added.

The Boy waited for the tour to continue.

"As you can see," the priest gestured, " . . . you have your own nightstand with a single drawer and a shelf underneath. You did bring a toiletry kit, did you not?" the priest asked.

The Boy remembered the black canvas zipping bag that his mother would have filled with his favorite toothpaste and soap if she hadn't been so sick. Instead, he had done it himself.

"Yes, sir," the Boy answered.

"Good," replied the priest, "because that's where it lives. In the morning, after you wash your face and brush your teeth, you will return it, wiped and dried, to its shelf. Your slippers belong under the nightstand while you sleep and either on your feet or in your appointed closet at all other times. Your towel hangs off the end of your bed and you will carry it to the shower and return it after use. As you will quickly discover, we are very strict about neatness and discipline around here." The priest paused and stared straight at the Boy. "Especially in my dorm," he emphasized.

The Boy fixated briefly on the leather strap that wrapped his waist and hung below his knees. He felt certain that the priest would not hesitate to use it.

"You will find that all actions have consequences, both good and bad, and it is far easier to follow the rules." The priest reached into a hidden fold of his smock. "Here is a key for your nightstand drawer," he explained as he handed it to the Boy, "though I assure you we have no issue with theft. It's more for you to gain a sense of responsibility for your own personal possessions."

The Boy placed the key in the lock on the drawer. "Responsibility," he remarked inwardly, "one of the Old Man's favorite words."

"A note of caution," the priest admonished. "I put Mariano at the end because he likes to have a tad too much fun sometimes, even though he's a nice boy. Now you are at the end, since you arrived last, next to Mariano. You'd do well not to be labeled part of his clan early on. Whenever there's trouble we question him immediately. He's usually involved and quite often the main instigator." The priest placed his palm on the Boy's mattress. "Drop your bags here and I'll take you to the dining hall. You can unpack later."

The Boy threw his duffel onto the bed and shuffled along the tile floor to the wooden corridors that wove their way through the monastery to the dining room.

The Boy heard the clinking and clanging of plates and silverware long before they turned the corner and pushed through the bat-wing doors that opened into the dining hall. Three sets of tables created six rows of boys facing each other. On a platform above them sat the priests, all sitting outward toward the boys, which seemed odd.

"Oh," the Boy realized, "it's to keep tabs on us." He started to sense the strong scrutiny and absently questioned it.

Father Jose María kindly pointed him toward a table where he took a seat and observed as a group of eight boys passed out the plates and then settled into their chairs.

A bell rang. The room fell quiet. A corpulent priest with horn-rimmed glasses stood and gave the blessing. After a communal "Amen" the noise resumed immediately.

"We call him '*Gordinflas*,'" a voice stated to the Boy's right, "'the Fat One.'" The Boy turned to his neighbor, a kid with a wide smile and playful demeanor. "You're the new kid, right?"

"Yes," the Boy said, "just got here."

The kid held out his hand to the Boy. "Good to meet you," the kid acknowledged. "I'm Mariano."

"Oh," the Boy exclaimed. "I have the bed next to you."

"I sort of figured that," Mariano joked, "since I used to have the last one. Now we're neighbors . . . " he laughed.

"Does everyone sit in the same place for each meal?" the Boy inquired, aware of what seemed to be a silent pecking order.

"Not necessarily," Mariano responded, "though it often happens that way. That's one of the few rules we don't have— and there's a lot of them." Mariano snorted through pursed lips like a horse. "Good idea to learn the main ones real fast. You get few second chances around here."

"One last fresh start . . . " flashed through the Boy's mind.

"Don't worry though," Mariano comforted. "I'll show you the ropes."

The Boy wondered if that was good or bad and remembered Father Jose María's warning.

The bell rang again. On cue the room came to its feet.

"Twenty minutes until class," ordered *Gordinflas*.

"C'mon," yelled Mariano, who darted out the door with the Boy in hot pursuit. They rushed through the corridors, down the stairs to the foyer, and out the front door. Once on the esplanade, Mariano sprinted across it, beckoning to the Boy as he ran. Panting, he stopped at the far corner and rested with his hands on his thighs to catch his breath. "The rule is, you can go anywhere on the esplanade as long as you can make it back through the main door within 60 seconds of the bell ringing."

The Boy noticed a strange bulge in Mariano's pocket.

"What are you hiding?" the Boy asked.

"Ah," Mariano exclaimed as he reached into his pants, "very observant." In his hand appeared a napkin from the dining room. "This, my friend, is rat bait."

The Boy peered closely as Mariano unwrapped the napkin to reveal a piece of cheese obviously pilfered from lunch.

"I'm about to show you the afternoon hunt," Mariano grinned. He waved his fingers toward the edge of the esplanade. "Do you see those holes over there?"

The Boy spotted the oblong openings that led under the sidewalk at the edge of the esplanade and appeared to be part of some type of drainage system. He nodded.

"That's the entry to the sewers," Mariano explained. "A.K.A., the rat house." He broke into an evil grin. "What we're going to do is to collect a few stones, put the cheese near the edge of the holes, back up about 10 meters, and wait for those suckers to come out. Then we'll pelt 'em with rocks. It's hilarious," Mariano concluded.

"Won't we get into trouble?" the Boy implored.

"No, man, that's the beauty of it." Mariano broke the cheese into pieces and strung it across the drainage openings. "The priests can't see us over in this corner and the only way we get caught is if someone pops around from the little chapel. That's where you come in. You keep watch while I try to nail a few and then we'll switch."

The Boy marveled at how little time it had taken him to find himself in this precarious position, almost as if he attracted trouble without seeking it. "Why me?" he pondered without an answer, at least partly aware of his dilemma.

"Missed him," Mariano squealed as a thrown rock clattered aimlessly down the drain pipe. "Did you see how big he was?"

Chapter Twenty-Eight   **185**

The Boy watched as a monstrous black rat poked his nose out and sniffed at the air. Mariano cocked his arm back, waited for the rat to climb out and waddle after the cheese, whipped his arm forward, and skipped the stone over the rat's tail.

"Dang," Mariano cursed. "Missed again. Problem is, you can't get too close or they'll smell you and they won't come out. You want to give it a try? Maybe your aim is better . . . "

At that moment, the bell rang. Mariano took off in the direction of the school, as did the Boy, relieved that he wasn't put on the spot. The memory of the bird falling from the branch still haunted him and even tossing rocks at rats held no appeal. Still, he didn't want to come across as a pansy and felt grateful that he wasn't forced to prove himself.

As he crossed the portal into the school, Father Jose María gave him a tough look. "It appears that you've met Mariano," he half-stated, half-asked.

"Yes, sir," the Boy muttered in the way familiar to him, oddly reminiscent of how he answered his father at home.

"I hope that's not a premonition," he thought and said no more.

Chapter Twenty-Nine

The Boy slid into the desk armed with a stack of paper and his special pen—a blue and white, fat plastic Bic that held four colored ink cartridges from which to choose. He had never written a letter—at least nothing more than the "Thank You" notes at Christmas or after a birthday that his mother made him finish before he could play with his gifts.

He felt awkward, as if he didn't know what to say or how to start.

"Dear Old Man,

This will be my first attempt at a real letter . . . "

The Boy stopped. "That sounds so lame," he voiced to himself as he crumpled the page in his fist. He squared the sheets in front of him.

"Dear Old Man,

It has been almost a month since I got here . . . "

He stopped again. "The Old Man knows that, you bozo . . . " he berated. His fingers curled around the second sheet, squeezed it into a ball, and dropped it on the floor to join its twin.

He exhaled a long, frustrated sigh.

"Just talk to him," he told himself, "like a friend."

The Old Man's words snuck into his consciousness. "Every master was once a rank amateur, Boy. The key is to begin and never quit . . . "

He switched colors from black to blue and willed his Bic to the blank page.

"Dear Old Man,

"It's colder here than in Altafulla, I guess because of the higher altitude and the lack of breeze from the Mediterranean. I miss the smell and our talks on Sundays and even the taste of the *menta.*

"I remember you telling me that when you had challenges that you would talk to your mentor in your mind and that he would help you figure things out. Well, I have a lot of time to think, especially at night because they turn the lights out at 9:30 PM, which is kind of early.

"I lie in bed with my hands behind my head and replay many of the conversations that we've had. It's funny because it seems that I missed what you were saying in person and am only just grasping it now—particularly if it was important, like when you tap your fingers on the bamboo (yes, I did notice that much).

"I don't quite get it. It seems like one should hear better in person than in playback. Anyway, I'm sure I've forgotten a few things and may need a reminder sometime.

"I almost got in trouble the other night with my friend Mariano, who is a bit of a prankster. He taught me a game called 'Catch the Bat.' There are thousands of them in the monastery and they fly through the hallways constantly, though usually much too high to snatch. If they don't sense any people, once in a while they will swoop down low, and Mariano hid behind an archway holding his jacket outstretched in front of him. As soon as a bat swooped by, he took three fast steps and pounced on it, trapped it in his jacket, and waited for it to stop squirming. Then he gathered it up and walked along the corridor until we ran into one of the tough guys—at which point Mariano flapped open his jacket and let the bat go. Scared the heck out of the kid—quite hilarious, actually—and we ran away to find another spot to try again.

"Father Jose María (my dorm master) spotted us while making rounds and asked us what we were doing. 'Playing hide and go seek,' Mariano fibbed immediately, and in that moment I decided I wouldn't do that anymore. If anything, all the priests' rules have helped show me the connection between actions and consequences in a weird kind of way. Around here, poor actions trap you and take away opportunities, where better actions give us privileges and create options and chances for adventure.

"I even heard that there's a real torture chamber in the basement somewhere that dates back to the Inquisition, with blood stains on the wall from centuries ago that have turned brown from oxidation. Only a handful of kids have ever seen it and I want to be one of them. Father Jose María told me that he would show me the secret entrance from the king's chambers into the chapel, through which his majesty could sneak in and out of mass whenever he wanted. I also want to climb up to the king's chair that is carved into the mountain stone and, to do that, I need to earn more privileges. Funny how a lot of the things you've said make more sense now.

"How are things at home?

"Have you caught any fish yet?

"I finished reading the *Count of Montecristo* the other day and I relate to what you told me about winning the battle in the mind first. The Count lost when he was confused and had to straighten things out inside before he could come back to victory. At first, I read super fast and wanted to know the whole story but, as I came closer to the end, I slowed down and only allowed myself a few pages each day so that I could make it last. Thanks again for the book. I enjoyed it a lot.

"I'm reading *Man of La Mancha* now and really like Don Quixote. Do you think he's a Great One? I'm not sure because he sometimes does goofy things like fight windmills.

"I'm sorry that I have to stop. In a few minutes they will call 'lights out' and I want to finish on time to send this tomorrow.

"Please write to me if you can and if your hands don't hurt too much.

"I'll be home for the Christmas holidays, though that feels awfully far away. Say 'hi' to the sea for me. I miss it, and you and my boat.

Your friend, "

The Boy signed the letter, carefully folded the sheets of paper, and slid them into the envelope. All of a sudden, it occurred to him that he didn't have an address. He sat clutching the envelope in silence as his eyes welled with tears until they burst and caused tiny streams to run down the sides of his nose, over his upper lip, and into his mouth.

He quashed a sniffle and kept his gaze on the ground, sequestered in his own private bubble of emotion.

Father Jose María crossed the study floor. "What's wrong?" he asked.

The Boy looked up. "I just wrote a letter to my friend, the Old Man, that I've told you about and I don't even have his address," he stammered through the tears that fell out of loneliness and frustration.

Father Jose María put his hand on the Boy's shoulder. He knew full well what precious few role models the Boy had ever had and the Old Man was certainly one of them—perhaps the only one.

"Maybe I can help you," Father Jose María offered.

"Really?" asked the Boy with a speck of hope.

"I can call the local priest, who undoubtedly knows everybody," Father Jose María explained. "I'll bet you he can get the address—if he doesn't have it already."

The Boy cheered up enough to stop crying. "Wow," he voiced. "That would be great."

"Get some rest," Father Jose María urged. "I bet I'll have that address within a day or two."

The Boy glanced down at the letter in his hand and flashed on the rocks and the sea and, most of all, his friend.

"I'll see you real soon, Old Man," he promised himself, "real soon."

Chapter Thirty

Nearly a month had passed since Father Jose María helped track down the Old Man's address. As the Boy strolled by the mail room on his way outdoors after lunch, he almost missed the tip of the envelope protruding from his mail slot. Long ago he had left behind the disappointment of checking for mail to no avail and, even now, believed that the tan packet must be misfiled and intended for someone else. He pulled it out to discover a red wax seal on the back—further proof that it couldn't be for him. Who could he know that had a seal?

He flipped it over to find his name on the front and, with his heart beating faster, slipped out the front door and across the esplanade to a solitary spot on the sidewalk. There he sat, drew a deep breath, and tucked his little finger into the corner of the crease, where he began to tear.

A strange yet familiar smell wafted from the envelope. The Boy paused, frowned, then yelped as it dawned on him: "The *menta*," he called out loud in recognition. With bursting anticipation, he extracted the two sheets and unfolded them to discover three pieces of the candy so full of memories resting within. He popped one into his mouth and turned his eyes to the page.

"Dear Boy,

"I hope you don't mind that I call you that in writing even if it seems more appropriate in person. I received your letter and, after reading it several times, have placed in a preferred place it in my top desk drawer.

"In a matter of weeks, it appears as though you have enjoyed your fair share of adventures, with even more to come. Congratulations!

"I had an adventure of my own the other day that I thought you'd want to hear. I was fishing on the rocks when all of a sudden my line goes taught and I'm sure I've caught the big one—except that it doesn't move like a fish. In fact, it doesn't move at all. I'm stressing and straining until finally I sense some give and am able to pull my capture to the surface. Do you know what it was? The inner tube of a motorcycle that must have been stuck on something on the bottom!

"I laughed and took it into town as a souvenir, where the old guys at the *bodega* shared a chuckle. I can see you laughing, too!

"I appreciate your insight on our conversations and agree with you completely. Not only do we not grasp a message fully the first time around, most of us need to hear the same thing over and over, from different perspectives and outlooks, before it will truly sink. We live so stuck in our beliefs, many of them mistaken, that rather than examine them or check them out, we defend them and find ways to justify our actions that conform to them. Far better to read and question, pay close attention to that which challenges our established ideas, and adopt only that which serves us after tireless examination.

"The Great Ones draw their own conclusions, Boy, as should you—no sleepwalking.

"As for Don Quixote—I'm not sure, though I can tell you that the author, Miguel de Cervantes, was a Great One without a doubt. When you finish, perhaps you might consider the work of García Lorca, another behemoth with advanced notions. I think you would gain from him as well. I consider books among my closest friends as well as humble servants that never let me down. Keep seeking, Boy, reading and thinking about what you read. Just because something is printed, that does not make it valuable, though some often draw that conclusion. Only you can determine what is best for you, and solely after much search and reflection. Live your own life, Boy, and be true to yourself.

"The waters have taken on their fall hues, the air carries a chill, and the days end sooner. Other than that, the sea remains unchanged and in that I find much beauty.

"I heard you would be back in a few weeks and look forward to our talks when you return.

"Please enjoy the *menta*. I'll have more waiting for you on the rocks.

"Your faithful friend,

The Old Man"

The Boy carefully folded the sheets and restored the letter to its envelope, which he clenched to his chest, as he had when the Old Man gave him the book.

He could visualize him perfectly, his dark-skinned wrinkle of a face, his gentle eyes, and calloused hands that nonetheless felt so soft when he applied the aloe. The Boy pictured him leaning forward, plucking his line before settling back, and adjusting the pole between his sandal-covered feet.

For a moment, he felt the warm rays of the sun brushing against his cheek and making him squint as he rolled his gaze across the copper-tinted water of the Mediterranean. The sea called to him and, even in absence, provided solace.

If for no more reasons than these, at least briefly, he longed for home.

Chapter Thirty-One

The Boy's face opened into a wide grin as he scuttled up the rocks to greet the Old Man.

"Catch any inner tubes lately?" he jested and they laughed and embraced.

"Good to see you, Boy," the Old Man replied. "It looks like you've grown a bit."

"Thanks for the *menta*," the Boy offered. "It reminded me of you and this place."

"Ah," the Old Man sighed happily, "I've brought you more." He removed a small bag from the sash around his waist. "So you could take some back to school."

"Thank you," the Boy repeated. He reached into his pocket and held his hand toward the Old Man. "I have something for you, too."

The Old Man accepted the object wrapped in tissue and quickly opened it.

"It's a key chain from El Escorial," the Boy shared, "I didn't know if you had one or not."

"From now on, I'll use this one," the Old Man declared, "to remind me of my friend."

The Boy settled onto his familiar spot as if he had been there forever.

"He gave us back our guns," the Boy began. "And he told me that I can use my boat in the spring."

"That's good," the Old Man answered. "Do you think it was because of your grades?"

"I don't know," the Boy said. "I guess so. I had only one 'B' and the rest 'A's."

"Remarkable what you can do when you apply yourself," the Old Man noted.

The Boy cast his glance downward. "Except that I'm not sure I want to return."

"We all must play our cards, Boy, you know that." The Old Man tapped his pole and cleared his throat before continuing. "When you step onto the field, whatever field that is, success lies in giving it all you've got. When you leave it all there, you walk off with your head high, every time. If you give less of yourself, you will not taste success, regardless of the final score. The Great Ones understand that the by-product of doing your best is that you will win far more often than you lose—though even then they know not to dwell in their victories, nor despair over defeats. Life is long and there will be plenty of challenges, obstacles, and diverse circumstances. Do your best and the scorecard will take care of itself—no matter where you are or what you face."

The Boy kept his gaze low, uncertain, and troubled by doubt.

"I come here all year long," the Old Man persisted, "because I love the seasons—the solitude in December and the crowds in July, the chill at Christmas and the suffocating heat in the summer, the way the days end earlier or later—so many things.

What experience has shown me is that winter always turns into spring and cold, harsh times give way to warmer, easier periods. I mentioned earlier that you'd grown, Boy, and I meant it in more ways than just size. I sense that your springtime may be near."

"He asked me to play tonight and I agreed," the Boy stated, "though I'm not really sure how I feel about that anymore."

"Give it all you have, Boy," the Old Man urged, "and, win or lose, stay humble. The Great Ones never flaunt their victories nor do they despair about the losses. Both victories and defeats give equal opportunity for reflection, introspection, and the seeds of wisdom. Do your best, accept the lessons, and let your hand play out in due course. If you do, the scorecard will take care of itself."

They lolled in quiet enjoyment of each others' company. The Boy flashed on the Old Man's words in the letter about the beauty in the unchanged. He vaguely observed as the Old Man stood to skirmish with an undetermined creature from the briny drink. He noticed himself clicking his sandals together out of habit. The perch felt as hard as before and the sea whispered with its waves. And yet, things had changed. Something had changed. Perhaps it was him, though he could not identify how. He wished the day would go on and on, for, as the sun slipped from the sky, he knew he would have to leave.

"I have to go soon," the Boy mumbled. "I don't want to make him mad."

"I know," the Old Man acquiesced. He stuck his arm far into his bag and dug out a package, which he handed to the Boy. "Merry Christmas," he said with a smile.

The Boy tore the wrapping off to find a book almost identical to the first one that the Old Man gave him before he left.

"It's another piece by Dumas," the Old Man explained. "Since you enjoyed the first one, I felt that you might benefit from this as well."

"*The Three Musketeers*," the Boy read out loud. "I've heard of this."

"Perhaps you can write to me and tell me what you learn from it," the Old Man suggested.

"Of course I will," the Boy promised. "I'll do it as soon as I finish with García Lorca—which I already started."

The Old Man nodded his approval. "Books that teach us and inspire us," the Old Man said, "become classics, read by generation after generation. Too many fill their minds with garbage and miss out on the joy of an eye-opening opportunity. The Great Ones are perpetual students, seeking constantly to better themselves."

The Boy dallied, not wanting to go, though he knew that to stay much longer would swamp him with emotion. He further knew that he did not want to cry.

"Time passes quickly, Boy," the Old Man reassured him. "In a matter of weeks you will be here again, and I will be waiting, as always."

The Boy shot one last glance at the sea, the sky, and his friend, the Old Man. He stood, turned, and started down the rocks. "Good luck with the fishing," he said and meant it.

The Old Man waved. "Head high, Boy, remember," he called out in farewell. "Hold your head high."

Chapter Thirty-Two

After class, the Boy and Mariano jogged down the esplanade at a fast clip.

"We need to get there right away," Mariano counseled, "or we'll never get a *pista*." He glanced sideways at the Boy. "Don't worry," he spluttered as they hurried, "I know a shortcut."

"Where?" the Boy asked.

Mariano gestured ahead. "By that big tree that rises higher than the wall. We climb up the first branch, over the top, and down the back side of the wall, using cracks that are already there for our hands and feet. Then we bolt across the formal gardens and squeeze through a hole in the fence, and voila—right next to the tennis courts without going all the way to the front entrance and having to boogie back up the hill to get a court. We'll save ourselves 15 minutes."

"I'm not sure," the Boy countered. "I don't want to lose any privileges."

Mariano threw him a strained look. "What?" he retorted. "That's bogus. You don't lose privileges unless you get caught—which we're not going to do."

The Boy wrestled with himself. What harm could there be in climbing down a wall even if it was out of bounds?

"Buck, buck, buck," Mariano taunted as he flapped his elbows up and down. "You're just chicken, that's all. Buck, buck, buck . . . "

The Boy so wanted to prove him wrong, to lead the charge over the wall, to show him what he could do and what he was made of. The forces of good and evil tore at this mind. "Actions have consequences, do the right thing, the scorecard will take care of itself," on and on.

"It's not that," he finally mumbled to Mariano without conviction. "I don't think it's a good idea. That's all."

"Yeah, right," Mariano jeered and shrugged his shoulders. "Buck, buck, super-chicken—see ya' on the other side, where I'll be playing and you'll be watching."

Mariano pulled himself onto the branch and disappeared in the foliage. The Boy walked toward the fields, angry at Mariano for goading him and even angrier at himself for getting stuck in a no-win situation. He shoved his hands into his pockets and ambled along the sidewalk as other boys rushed by to claim a court. He didn't care.

A distant scream snapped him out of his bubble. "Was that Mariano?" he wondered, spun on his boot, and bolted to the big tree. He hauled himself up and poked his head over the top of the wall. Fifteen meters below, on the ground, completely still, lay Mariano.

"Is he dead?" the Boy worried and in an instant a familiar memory flooded his mind, the image of his little brother after the pellet gun shot. "They're going to blame me," he told himself. "Now what do I do?"

Chapter Thirty-Two   **201**

He sprinted toward the school. Fifty meters from the door he spotted Father Jose María speaking with a classmate.

"Father," he yelled. "It's Mariano. He fell off the wall. He's not moving," the Boy uttered between gasps.

"Whoa! Slow down, son," Father Jose María dictated. "What are you saying?"

In clipped bursts the Boy explained: "We were going to play tennis, and we knew we had to get there fast to grab a *pista*, and Mariano said he knew a shortcut, and he wanted me to go with him, but I didn't want to, so he went ahead and then I heard a scream and I went back to check and he fell and he's lying there on the ground right now . . . " The Boy blurted out his words.

Father Jose María's voice turned to stone. "Show me where—exactly," he commanded.

The Boy pointed across the esplanade. "All the way at the end—the huge tree in the middle."

"I'll take it from here," Father Jose María ordered, "and, in the meantime, you get yourself back inside and wait for me in detention hall."

"But . . . " the Boy protested.

Father Jose María cut him off with an icy look as he broke into a run.

The Boy plodded toward the school, disgusted. Fat lot of good that did to help his friend. Big benefits for stepping up. What a crock.

A few hours later, Father Jose María entered the room and crossed to the Boy, where he took a seat at the table next to him.

"How's Mariano?" the Boy inquired.

"He'll be fine—though he has a nasty bruise on his head," Father Jose María replied. "No broken bones that we could find. He knocked himself out and we're keeping him in the infirmary for observation."

The Boy shook his head.

"I did talk to him after the doctor finished," Father Jose María continued, "and it seems as though I owe you an apology."

"Oh?" the Boy mumbled, a tad perplexed.

"It takes a lot of courage to stand up to peer pressure," Father Jose María praised, "especially as a newcomer without many friends. Not many would have done what you did."

The Boy sensed a hint of a smile take over the corners of his mouth.

"Around here, that type of behavior carries its own rewards. I'm proud of you for what you did, and for looking after Mariano." Father Jose María held out his hand. "I'm sorry for my harsh tone and for doubting you. I was wrong."

The Boy shook hands and smiled wide at the priest, who smiled back.

"Do you remember the first day you arrived when I picked you up at the train station?" Father Jose María put his hand on the Boy's biceps.

"Yes, sir," the Boy admitted. "I do."

"On that day I promised you that we would begin by believing the best of you. I strive to trust in the positive and welcome disappointment when someone lets me down rather than assume the worst and apologize when someone does what's right." The priest squeezed the Boy's arm. "Today, I did not do that. Through your actions, you reminded me of that lesson, for which I'm grateful. Thank you," he concluded.

"You're welcome," the Boy said, beaming.

"This weekend is a *puente*—three days—and most of the kids will be gone. I was planning on hiking up the mountain to the king's chair with a picnic and wondered if you might like to join me?"

The Boy's eyes lit up even brighter. "Yes, sir," he exclaimed right away. "Yes, sir, I would."

Father Jose María stood up to leave. "Excellent," he concluded. "Oh, and you're off detention. You shouldn't have been here in the first place."

The priest left and the Boy remained, caught in a mosaic of emotions, replaying the events of the day: the offer, the refusal, the disappointment, the anger, the accident, the denial, the punishment, the forgiveness, the reward, and his own pride and elation in the aftermath.

Would it always be this hard and complicated? Could he ever reach a space where decisions flowed easily without torment or second-guessing, without pressure and never-ending doubt? He would ask the Old Man, he determined. He would write him another letter.

That night, alone at the end of the long row of beds in his dormitory, he slept a different kind of sleep. He dreamt of his boat, the hum of the hull as it glides in resonance across the waves, the warm bake of the sun high in the sky, the faraway horizon that knows no bounds, the fleeting, momentary feeling of peace and harmony that comes over him when effort becomes effortless and all it takes is an able navigator, a taut sail, and a smooth breeze.

He slept and in his dream the navigator was he.

Chapter Thirty-Three

The Boy slipped into the far-right corner of the study hall room after dinner. He reached into his bag for his writing paper and his book, which he placed in front of him on the desk. Without regard to those around him, he chose blue on his Bic and began to compose.

"Dear Old Man,

"Thanks again for *The Three Musketeers*. I started reading it last week and, so far, D'Artagnan is my favorite. He has such an independent spirit and goes his own way, even though he is also a leader. I haven't gotten very far yet so maybe that will change. I'll let you know.

"I had an interesting episode happen yesterday and was hoping that you might help me answer a few questions that keep coming up. My friend Mariano invited me to take a shortcut out of school bounds on our way to the playing fields and, when I declined, he went ahead anyway. The problem was that he fell climbing down a wall and, when I went to get help for him, I was assigned equal blame and sent to detention even though I was innocent. Fortunately, Mariano fessed up—no, he wasn't badly hurt—and Father Jose María apologized and let me go.

"What I want to know is this: Do you ever get to a space where decisions become clear and happen naturally or, if not naturally, without constant fear or worry about the repercussions? D'Artagnan makes his mind up in an instant and, even when he makes mistakes, he moves on quickly without second-guessing. Is that normal, or only in a story? It wasn't easy to turn down Mariano's offer and, even when I did, I questioned myself. I'd be grateful if you could shed some light on this.

"Father Jose María invited me to hike up to the king's chair this weekend, which I guess is kind of a privilege. Only four kids are going and he said that we might climb to the summit if the weather cooperates. I hope we can because there's snow up there and I've never felt real snow. I was glad he invited me even though I know it was part of his effort to say he was sorry for punishing me without reason. In any case, I'm included and that's what matters.

"I have my tickets for Easter already and arrive the evening of Good Friday. I look forward to seeing you at the usual time on the rocks on Sunday afternoon.

"Thanks again for the *menta*. I still have a few pieces and I save them for when I feel lonely to use as a pick me up. It may sound weird, but in the taste I sometimes smell the sea as if I were there with you.

"I'll write again about the Musketeers and, when you have time, if you could give me your opinion on my questions, I would really appreciate it. Thanks in advance.

"Please tell Pedro I said 'hi' if you see him.

"Your good friend,"

The Boy scribbled a signature, stuffed the letter in the envelope that was already stamped, and sat staring absently at the space before him in somber reflection. It hadn't been so bad being apart—the priests behaved fairly and seldom singled anyone out unless they deserved it. He could make his own mark here, based on his own actions, which gave him a certain freedom. He missed his little brother, the Old Man, and sometimes fresh cooking, although even bad food in good company seemed better than a gourmet meal heaped with abuse. He wondered if he would be back next year, whether they would keep him in Altafulla, or if he would have a choice, and he asked himself whether his father enjoyed having him far away as much as he liked being far from them. He found that idea slightly odd, though drew no further conclusions from it. He did want to be home in the summer, when he could escape in his boat and spend more time with the Old Man.

Almost unconsciously, his hand drew the book to him, which he opened to the page where he had left off, marked by the Old Man's letter. Until the bell rang, he read and dreamt of olden days, and honor and swordsmen and swashbucklers topped by felt hats with long plumes. He experienced courage, abhorred the traitors, fought the battles in his imagination, and let the words form impressions that one by one shaped his character without his knowledge.

On the other side of the country, the Old Man thought of him fondly as he twisted strands of twine to fix his fishing pole. He smiled at the memories, sighed over the foibles, contemplated without effort the role he played in it all, and comfortably awaited his return.

Chapter Thirty-Four

The Boy's face broke into a wide smile as he spied the brown envelope and pulled it from his mail slot to reveal a second red seal. He stepped out the front door and crossed the stone courtyard to a tree he discovered beyond the sidewalk that had a smooth root that, along with the trunk, made a perfect cradle in which to sit. He opened the letter.

"Dear Boy,

"I hope you had a grand excursion to the king's chair and that your adventure leads to many more. Take advantage of all that is out there and don't waste a chance to see something new—a museum, a ball game, an outdoor concert—every opportunity offered. All of these will help you become well rounded and expose you to different ideas and perceptions from which to form your own.

"I was quite pleased to receive your letter and the questions it contained. It shows that you are becoming a seeker and seekers seldom sleepwalk. I will do my best to answer you although only your own experiences will ultimately shape your character, and it is strength of character that creates clarity, decisiveness, and lack of fear. Every thought you think, every word you say, and all of your actions leave a mark and serve to weaken or solidify your beliefs. That is why it is crucial to read of the Great Ones and learn their philosophies. Most sleepwalkers fall prey to poor ways of thinking because that is all they are exposed to. While all of us are influenced by those around us and what we allow in our minds, a select few understand this fully and guard carefully who they associate with, what they watch, whose words they heed, and so on. The rest fall victim to the views shown on television and espoused in cheap tabloids, whose sole purpose is to provide an escape into a fantasy that somehow seems more appealing than real life.

"Think about what you read, think about the consequences of your actions, and even think about what you are thinking about. Is it serving you? Is it leading you where you want to go, or is it simply a distraction? Then act accordingly. The Musketeers repeat over and over the motions that make them master swordsmen, until the actions become automatic. This is the way of a master. Competence leads to confidence and competence comes from repetition. This is one of the keys to your question. Go out and live and in so doing acquire experience, which, coupled with evaluation and scrutiny, will lead to wisdom—and more confidence. There is no quick fix and you can't shortcut the process.

"Above all, understand this (and I will tell you that I have been waiting for the right moment to share this with you): There are two fundamental virtues, which in my mind form the core of all success, without which all else is moot. They are tenacity and perseverance and form the bedrock of a successful life. No brilliant strategy will ever beat the person who simply refuses to give up. No clever plan, no grandiose scheme, no cutting-edge idea—nothing can defeat the man or woman who doesn't know how to quit. Of all the ideas we have shared, to me this is the most important. As the saying goes, 'winners never quit and quitters never win.'

"If you truly want to forge a character that frees you from fear and self-doubt, take this lesson to heart more than any other: The Great Ones never quit, Boy. NEVER!

"You will find that winners make decisions quickly and change their minds slowly. Fools take forever to make up their minds and then change them again quickly. There can be no success on that path. We will speak of this in person when you come home, for it is paramount.

"I spoke with Pedro and he sends his greetings. He told me to let you know that the *Club Marítimo* would open for Easter and that he would have your boat ready. He also mentioned that they were seeking another worker for the high season, in case you might be interested. Personally, I think it would be good for you to have a summer job and earn your own income. If you go to him first, I'm sure you can get the position.

"I will see you in a few weeks and we will talk more. Until then I remain . . .

"Your faithful friend,

The Old Man"

The Boy froze in stillness absorbing the Old Man's words. He marveled at the ferocity with which they leapt off the page and could think of no other time when the Old Man had expressed himself so strongly, except maybe when he told the story after shooting his brother. "Why was this so important?" he asked himself again and again.

"Don't worry, Old Man," he told himself silently, "I'm not a quitter and I won't let you down, regardless of the reasons."

He would read the letter once more later and many times after that, almost as if to find the hidden meaning or the secret that the Old Man wanted him to absorb more than anything—a secret that, unknowingly, he had already found.

Chapter Thirty-Five

The Old Man waved as the Boy started his ascent up the rocks.

"That's odd," the Boy noted, joyful to see his friend. "Why is he standing up?"

As he drew closer the Boy discovered a curious smirk on the Old Man's face, as if he couldn't erase it even if he wanted to.

"What's up, Old Man?" the Boy blurted out, instead of hello.

The Old Man opened his hands to reveal two long pieces of aloe in each palm, the left one mixed with blood from a nasty cut and the right one half-covered by an ugly blister.

"I had quite a tussle a little while ago," the Old Man shared. "Almost did me in."

"With a fish?" the Boy snorted in disbelief.

"Indeed," the Old Man replied, "and a courageous and noble beast he was. That's why my line is out of the water."

The Boy spied the Old Man's fishing pole cradled against the rocks along with an ancient wooden lure with slightly faded colors.

"What happened?" the Boy inquired, incredulous.

"Take a seat and I'll tell you," the Old Man said.

The Boy climbed onto his spot. The Old Man took his place next to him, then began.

"Do you think dogs like bones?" the Old Man asked.

"Yes," the Boy answered in a questioning tone.

"Seriously," the Old Man insisted, "do you think dogs like bones?"

"Of course they do," the Boy retorted, a tad annoyed. "Dogs love bones."

"No they don't," the Old Man corrected. "Dogs like steak. Dogs get bones, so that's what they eat. If you throw a dog a bone or a piece of steak, he's going after the steak every time."

The Boy frowned. "So?" he grunted.

"Most people spend their lives chasing after bones," the Old Man clarified. "Personally, I'd rather be a bit more patient, work a bit harder, and earn myself the right to order a steak."

"What in the world does that have to do with fishing?" the Boy demanded.

The Old Man picked up his lure and held it between his thumb and forefinger.

"I carved this lure about 35 years ago." He turned it over and thrust it toward the Boy. "As you can see, it has four holes in which to screw a hook. The kind of fish I'm going after strike their bait from behind. If you place your hook near the back of the lure, you have a better chance to catch a lot of fish. On the other hand, if you place it near the front, as I have, then only the biggest fish can ever get hooked because they have to swallow the whole lure to reach the hook. The small fish will still strike the lure, but all they taste is a mouthful of wood. Does that make sense?"

The Boy furrowed his brow, still confused.

"I'm not interested in going after small fish," the Old Man stated simply. He unscrewed the hook, stuck it into a fold of his wide cloth belt, and placed the lure in his bag.

The Boy hesitated before speaking. "Does that mean that whenever I've watched you tug on your pole all you were doing was getting rid of little fish?"

"Pretty much," the Old Man acknowledged. "These old hands don't have many fights left in them, and I certainly didn't want to waste any on small fry."

"Wow," the Boy told himself quietly, as he reflected on the many inept and inappropriate fishing jokes he had made at the Old Man's expense. A shade of shame crept over him.

"Each of us has limited time and energy to go after our desires. Most people waste both without care or even awareness. The Great Ones know when to say 'no,' how to avoid distractions and temptations, and how to stay focused on what matters—big goals and dreams. Not only that," the Old Man continued, "the journey to greatness by definition means fighting bigger battles and facing greater challenges. The accomplishments themselves are mere by-products of who you become in the process. The glory of the moment is fleeting and transient. The confidence, pride, and belief in what you can do stay with you forever. Fighting the great fight, in that sense, is more important than winning."

"Do you really believe that, Old Man?" the Boy contested. "Or are you just saying it because you lost the fish?"

The Old Man looked down at him in fondness. The Boy wondered if he had pushed too far.

"Walk with me," the Old Man suggested. The Boy complied. They rose together and started across the rocks.

The Old Man pointed at a piece of line wedged into a crevice that trailed downward into the sea.

"Brace yourself so that you can handle the weight," the Old Man directed, "then pull that line up for me."

The Boy spread his legs, crouched down, and began to raise the line hand over hand.

"It's heavy," the Boy admitted, and, in that exact moment, the iridescent and sparkling scales of the front half of a large fish broke the surface.

"It's a fish," the Boy screamed, his eyes as big as saucers. "It's huge, almost as big as me . . . "

"Like I said earlier," the Old Man repeated, " . . . he put up one heckuva' battle. When I finally brought him in, I ran a line through his mouth and out of his gill so that he could stay alive and well until you arrived."

The Boy stared at the fish, mesmerized.

"What do you mean, Old Man? Why did you have to protect the fish? Aren't you going to keep him?"

"No, Boy," the Old Man responded. "I only fish for sport—to find out if I can still outfox a wily monster like this and if these ancient hands have what it takes. The local fishermen need him far more than I do and once we let him go perhaps he will find his way into their daily catch. He lives to fight another battle . . . " The Old Man paused. "Who knows, maybe it will be with you."

"But what are you going to tell your buddies, Old Man?" the Boy implored. "How will they believe you actually caught it if you don't show them?"

"I don't need to tell them anything, Boy," the Old Man assured. "It is enough that I know, and that I shared this moment with you."

The Old Man removed his *navaja* from his waistband, opened the blade, and cut the line. With a single thrust of the tail the fish disappeared.

"I can't believe it," the Boy blurt out, still reeling—both over the catch and the release.

"It's not that complicated, Boy," the Old Man urged. "If you study hard, you get good grades. If you lift weights, you build muscles. If you set the right hook, don't fall prey to distractions, and fish for long enough, you're bound to catch something big."

The Old Man issued a happy sigh. "Success in life lies in simple fundamentals. The sad reality is that most people fail to realize how close they are to succeeding when they quit. Such a fine line exists between success and failure, where one tiny extra effort can mean the difference between victory and defeat, between achieving a goal or having all the efforts that led up to that point go for naught over one last instance of neglect."

"I'll never stop, Old Man," the Boy boasted. "I want to be like the Great Ones."

"That may take some time, Boy," the Old Man cautioned. "Though if you apply yourself and do the work, I'm sure you can get there."

"I'm never going to quit," the Boy claimed, pushing his chest out. "Just like you and the fish. You can be sure of it."

The Old Man turned to him. "If you learn only that, my work is complete," he said in a soft tone. "Speaking of which, did you get your report card?"

The Boy nodded. "Brought it home Friday. All As. He told me last night that if I kept my grades up this last quarter, I could stay home next fall." A shadow fell over the Boy's brow. "Though, with the exception of you, my brother, and my boat, I'm not sure why I'd want to."

The Old Man patted him on the back. "Either way, it's good to have the choice, Boy, especially since you earned it based on your own diligence." The Old Man rested his hand on the Boy's shoulder. "I'm very proud of you."

That same surge of warmth he had felt once before washed over the Boy like a wave. He basked in the moment then snapped his head toward the Old Man. "I'm proud of you, too, Old Man," the Boy effused with excitement, "you caught an enormous fish!"

"There have been others before," the Old Man said quietly, "though perhaps none so significant as this."

The Boy wondered what he meant, though he let the comment lie, content to be with his friend and enjoy the breeze in quiet celebration. They spoke without words and he drew much strength from their conversations, a bond forged through friendship, hardships, and the many afternoons on the rocks.

"Let's go have an *helado* at the ice cream shop on the beach," the Old Man exclaimed suddenly. "I feel like celebrating."

The Boy carried the Old Man's bag and pole. As they crossed the sand side by side, the Boy felt little sorrow over leaving, content to revel in the joy of their moments together on such a momentous day.

"Thanks for the cone, Old Man," the Boy expressed. "I'll be back as soon as school gets out."

"Head high," the Old Man reminded as the Boy skipped away. "Travel well."

The Boy smiled at his fortune to have such a friend as he made his journey up the tall hill toward the church square. It was his most treasured joy and made him want to be better, to leave his mark, prove himself, and do his best, as if he were part of a cause much greater than himself. He reflected on *The Three Musketeers*, how they trusted and relied upon each other and, in so doing, found courage, power, and strength.

"I'll never let you down, Old Man," the Boy promised himself. "I swear it."

And, in that moment, as if to punctuate their agreement, the bells in the church tower began their evening toll.

Chapter Thirty-Six

The Boy finished his homework and pushed his schoolbooks aside in favor of the writing paper he kept in his bag.

"Dear Old Man,

"I finally understand what you meant about 'my space' when you told me that you wouldn't join me for a sail on my boat. I didn't get it back then and felt disappointed, but now, as I wonder whether to come back here to school after summer, it makes much more sense. This has become my space, too, a place where I can make my way without being scared, stand on my own two feet, and create something to be proud of. I'm not sure that I want to give that up. Maybe you can shed some light on this when I see you.

"I had a great experience last weekend on my second excursion with Father Jose María. Out of nine boys, I was the only underclassman invited and we hiked up the highest peak behind the cross at the Valley of the Fallen. It's amazing how an object that looks so huge from below can seem so small from above—all a matter of perspective, I guess. I decided that I wanted to stick with the lead group, which was really tough because two of the older boys had been up the trail before and were almost running to get to the top before anyone else. I had to push super hard to keep up and remind myself over and over not to quit as my muscles screamed at me. It was worth it because we made it long before the main group and had a chance to sit and gaze over the valley for quite a while. I know you would have appreciated the view.

"Thanks for the conversation we had even though you weren't here. My friend Mariano asked me to explore the underground pipe system with him and while he was talking I briefly asked myself what you would counsel. In a microsecond all the usual phrases popped in my head—'let others lead small lives, do the right thing, actions have consequences' and so on—which was sound advice and I was glad I said 'no' because Mariano stepped in a puddle of sewage and couldn't get rid of the smell before coming back. They stuck him in front of Saint Agustín, probably the worst punishment you can get around here, where you have to kneel on a stone courtyard in the middle of the night by yourself and do penance while the bats fly back and forth—and there are lots of them! Plus, if I had gone with him, I'm sure I would have been excluded from the hike. So, thanks for our talk.

"Thanks also for helping me get that job this summer at the *Club Marítimo*. I decided not to work on Sunday afternoons even though it's a busy day so that it won't cut into our time together. I was hoping that you could do me a favor and teach me how to fish. I never wanted to in the past, but, after you caught such a fine one, I started thinking about it. I'm not sure that I'm a fisherman but, since it's important to you, I want to find out why. Even if it took a while, I'm confident that I can pull one in eventually, if I stick with it—and I'd like to know what that feels like.

"I'm going to end now so that I can read a bit before 'lights out.' I picked up *Lazarillo de Tormes*, one of the only anonymous classics, recommended by four or five of the other boys. If I decide to come back here in the fall, I'll see if I can borrow it from the library and bring it home so that you can read it, too! I'll let you know if it's worth it once I finish.

"Don't empty the sea of all the big fish before I get there. See you on the rocks . . . "

The Boy flourished a signature and relished a smile for a few moments as he visualized the Old Man with his curious grin on the last day he saw him, the day he landed the fish. He decided right then that he would write to his little brother, especially since he was taking the brunt of their father's ire in the Boy's absence. He wondered why he hadn't thought of that earlier.

"Better late than never," the Boy rationalized. "Maybe a letter will encourage him like the Old Man's notes do for me."

He went to bed happy and at ease, rode the high seas on a little red boat, and dreamt of the day when, with his own bamboo pole, standing on the rocks, he hooked his first fish.

Chapter Thirty-Seven

Father Jose María pushed back from the table when he got the call over the loud speaker. He left the dining hall, returned a few minutes later, and crossed to the Boy, where he placed his palm on the Boy's shoulder.

"Telephone for you," he declared in a strained voice. "Follow me."

As they hurried down the corridor to the main office, the Boy spoke out. "Who is it?" he asked.

"Your mother," the priest answered. "She needs to speak with you."

"That's strange," the Boy told himself. "She has never called before . . . "

Father Jose María handed him the phone.

"Hello . . . " the Boy uttered into the receiver.

"Hello, son," came the reply and instantly the Boy's guard went up. She never called him "son" unless something was wrong.

"What's up?" he questioned cautiously.

"I have some bad news," she said, "and I don't quite know how to tell you." The Boy heard the puff of her inhaler. "Your friend, the Old Man, is no longer with us."

The Boy's chest collapsed. A vice gripped his lungs and heart and began to squeeze. "Nooo," he gasped.

"He passed away last night," she added softly.

"Noooo . . . " he whimpered as his face contorted in agony and the tears sprung forth.

"I'm sorry," she offered.

In a daze, the Boy, for an instant, ceased the sobs. "Can I . . . " he stammered, "can I come . . . ?" The words failed him.

"Yes," she responded. "I'll make the arrangements with Father Jose María. The ceremony is on Saturday . . . "

The Boy heard only her agreement. He mumbled a request to step outside as he gave the phone to the priest, who nodded his assent.

The Boy stumbled through the front door into a world that he no longer recognized, a world that made no sense, where all bright colors turned dim, all sounds were silenced, and all he could feel was pain.

Chapter Thirty-Eight

The train clickety-clacked across the high plains of Castilla in the direction of the Costa Dorada. Kilometer after kilometer, the tears ebbed and flowed, much like the rolling hills that appeared and disappeared one province after another. Almost in a trance, the Boy transferred platforms in Valencia and fell into a solitary booth as the North-bound train left the station. The city yielded to the country and its coast line and, soon, the vast Mediterranean stretched from side to side through his window. It looked placid, dark, and empty—nothing like the sea he remembered.

His father met him in Tarragona, where he hugged his little brother, who had nothing to say. Few words exchanged on the ride home, nor through dinner, for which the Boy was grateful. He lay in the top bunk in his room and stared at the ceiling, drunk with dull anguish, until, delirious with exhaustion, his eyelids slipped for a few restless hours of sleep, punctuated by nightmares and bouts of cold sweat.

The Boy had never seen so many people gathered in the square, not even for the biggest annual fiestas. He knew most of the locals though many were strangers he didn't recognize including an obviously important bishop who arrived in a limousine to conduct the service. The Boy sat alone in a dark pew in the very back. Through the drone of the bishop's voice, he could not erase an image of the Old Man fishing, tapping the bamboo with his finger, plucking the line with his left hand, and adjusting the pole in his feet—an image that played over and over without reprieve.

He followed the crowd out of the church's main entrance, where the local father stood greeting mourners solemnly and passing out the *menta*, the same menta that the Old Man had, in the same wrappers and purchased from the same store. Except that it wasn't the same. It wasn't the same at all and the Boy wanted none of it.

He strayed near the rear of the procession that wove its way through the streets of Altafulla to the cemetery where the bishop offered his final blessing. As the group dissipated, he found himself pulled toward the grave like a moth to a flame, unable to resist. He approached the mountain of dirt, forced himself to look down in the hole, where all he found was a polished pine box without a face. Again, he struggled to understand, to find any meaning to any of it.

"We came upon this in his pocket," a voice said off to his right.

He glanced over to discover the Old Man's youngest niece, who he recognized from many functions in the town.

"I think he would want you to have it," she continued as she thrust her closed fist in his direction and opened it to reveal the keychain from El Escorial that the Boy had given the Old Man.

"You were always his favorite," she added with a broken smile and a twinge of jealousy.

The Boy took the object, gazed blankly into her eyes, and uttered the only five syllables he could manage.

"He was a Great One," he stated before the tears clamped his mouth shut.

"There's something else," the girl tacked on, "if you could maybe walk me home."

In silence, the Boy escorted her past the bakery, the *bodega*, and down a narrow cobble-stoned corridor to an arch-shaped wooden door that swung inward into a courtyard. The girl gestured toward a bench against the wall.

"We think he would want you to have that, too," she offered in a kind and gentle voice.

The Boy followed her arm to the bench. On it, as he recognized immediately, lay the Old Man's fishing pole.

"Take it," the girl urged. "It's yours now."

The Boy's tears kept him from speaking though he nodded his head and knew that his thanks came through. He gripped the bamboo in one hand, the plastic bag with the gear in the other, and stumbled through the archway into the street, flooded by another wave of sorrow.

Clutching the pole, he wandered through the town without direction until he exhausted the streets and came to the foot of the hill of the cross. He plodded upward using the bamboo as a cane, reached the summit, collapsed to cry some more until, finally, the well dried up, the sobbing ceased, and numbness, once again, became his friend.

Epilogue

The Boy placed the pole in the Old Man's spot along with his Adidas bag that housed the fishing gear given to him by the Old Man's family. He took his customary place and stared blankly at the water, reliving the memories of the Old Man through images that played in rapid sequence across his imagination.

He sat and clicked his sandals together, past the pain, though certainly not over the hurt.

He knew what he had to do.

He knew and yet he didn't know how to begin exactly.

And so he sat, as the words came to him.

"Let others play small . . ."

"Winter never fails to turn into spring . . ."

"Leave it all on the field . . . no regrets . . ."

Steadily, the resolve grew from his core.

"I'll never quit, Old Man," the Boy muttered under his breath.

He stretched into his bag and pulled out the wooden lure along with a piece of cloth that he had wrapped around the hook. He held the line in his hand, with the four holes facing upward, and remembered, in vivid detail, his last day with the Old Man, the aloe mixed with blood, the curious grin, the ice cream on the beach, and, most of all, that huge monster. He jammed the hook into the farthest hole, just like the Old Man, and tightened it down.

"I'm coming after you, big fish," the Boy spewed with ferocity.

He attached the lure to his line. The fury built within him.

"Hold your head high, Boy." The memory of the Old Man reached across the ethers.

He forced his gaze upward, rose to his feet, picked up the pole, and with the Old Man's words echoing in his ears stepped forth, into the space that, until that instant, had always been the Old Man's.

For a moment, time ceased. He saw the sea, the same sea it had always been only different, older somehow. He tasted the salty air and it, too, carried a new flavor in its breeze. He squinted into the giant sun that bore down on him with a blazing heat he did not remember.

Suddenly, just ahead under the surface, the Boy caught a glimmer of movement. He strained his neck forward to see a fish rise to the surface, so massive that the Boy, for a full second, spied only the dorsal fin and part of the body as it glided in an arch through the water.

"It's the spirit of the Old Man," the Boy cried out loud. "But what's he trying to tell me?"

The answer sprang to his mind.

"Pay it forward, Boy," spoke the silent voice. "The Great Ones always do . . ."

The Boy stood still as a statue, frozen by the message and its implications, transfixed on the dark sea in which the giant fish had disappeared.

Unconsciously, his left palm found its way to his chest, where it covered the key chain that hung from his neck above his heart.

"I'll do it for you, Old Man," he vowed.

From deep within that dark repository of bottomless power, he gathered all his strength. In slow motion, with an iron-willed purpose, he cocked his arms backwards, called forth his rage, and tapped his driving ire as he cemented his pledge to honor the Old Man's parting wish. In one giant release, the Boy cast the ancient lure far into the Mediterranean.

As the line settled, out of the corner of his eye he detected a flicker of motion on the shore below and turned his head.

For the very first time, scrambling up the rocks, came his little brother.

The End

Notes from the Author

www.TheGreatOnesOnline.com

Much like Jim Rohn affirmed in his gracious foreword, I believe that the union of a mentor and disciple or student represents not only one of life's greatest joys, but also a proven method to assure and accelerate success in all aspects of life. I shudder to think where I would be today without the mentors who have so positively influenced me over the past four decades. The terms *lost, miserable*, and certainly *broke* come to mind.

Whether for fitness or for writing, speaking or managing assets, love languages or parenting, we can seek out mentors for everything. Who better to help us along than the person who has successfully traveled the path we wish to follow?

If this book accomplishes anything, I hope that it will inspire you to find your own mentors, learn from them, and embrace the philosophies of *The Great Ones*—and they are out there, if you seek them.

In that regard, I urge you to visit our website www.The GreatOnesOnline.com and learn from the industry giants that have shared their stories with us. There are lots of free materials, ezines, videos, and much more to support you in your quest for greatness.

We all need a support team. There is no reason whatsoever to make so significant a journey as life itself alone.

Wishing you fabulous health, boundless prosperity, and overflowing happiness,

Ridgely

About the Author

Author/speaker **Ridgely Goldsborough** (known in Latin America as "Richeli") has written eight books in the last five years and produces a column entitled "A VIEW FROM THE RIDGE" that is read across North America and around the world on over 30,000 websites (in Spanish it is titled "Revista Richeli").

He is the television show host and creator of the acclaimed series *Modest to Millions*—a program that chronicles the principles of prosperity, success, and wealth accumulation according to self-made individuals who began from modest backgrounds and went on to extraordinary achievements (now also an internet phenomenon).

Ridgely is a widely sought after speaker on prosperity and wealth principles in person, on radio and television, and via the internet, in both English and Spanish.

After law school and a number of years in business, Ridgely began his professional career as the publisher of the *Upline Journal*, a monthly periodical for the direct sales industry. He then founded *Network Marketing Lifestyles* magazine, a four-color glossy publication distributed by Time-Warner, and subsequently *Domain Street Magazine*, the first publication of the domain names industry. He has written hundreds of articles, hosted his

235

own weekly radio show, and is a frequent television guest. His client list includes YPO, EO, the U.S. Government, most of the major DSA companies, and dozens of corporations.

Ridgely attended the University of Virginia as an undergraduate and Whittier College School of Law for his graduate work, and he is a member of the Bar Association of California. In addition, he holds a Master Writers' Certificate from UCLA. He lives in Florida with his wife Kathy and their four children.

www.AViewFromTheRidge.com

www.Richeli.com (Spanish)